EXTRA ORDINARY WOMEN

A History of the Women's Institutes

*"The WI offers opportunities for all women
to enjoy friendship, to learn, to widen their
horizons and together to influence local,
national and international affairs."*
WI Mission Statement

EXTRA ORDINARY WOMEN

A History of the Women's Institutes
by Gwen Garner

WI BOOKS

DEDICATION

To all the WI friends I have gained during my 37 years' membership, and the Federations and Institutes where I made them.

My grateful thanks to all the people who talked to me, sent me information, newsletters and year books, and particularly to Marguerite Shaw and Tracy Sortwell for the preliminary work on the questionnaire sent to WIs.

A special thank you to my patient husband who constructively questioned every word I wrote.

Gwen Garner

Copyright © National Federation of Women's Institutes
First Published 1995 by WI Books Ltd
in association with Southgate Publishers Ltd
Glebe House, Church Street, Crediton, Devon EX17 2AF

British Library Cataloguing in Publication Data.
A CIP catalogue record for this book is available from the British Library.

ISBN 0 947990–12–7

Printed and bound in Great Britain by BPC Wheaton Ltd, Exeter, Devon.

CONTENTS

Members from the Cambridge Federation taking part in a gliding course at the University Gliding Club, Duxford.

WHAT IS THE WI?
A message from the National Federation of Women's Institutes.

IF YOU enjoy this book, the chances are that you would enjoy belonging to the largest women's organization in the country – the Women's Institute. We are friendly, go-ahead, like-minded women, who derive enormous satisfaction from all the movement has to offer. The list is long – you can make new friends, have fun and companionship, visit new places, develop new skills, take part in community services, fight local campaigns, become a WI market producer, and play an active rôle in an organization which has a national voice.

The WI is the only women's organization in the country which owns an adult education establishment. At Denman College, you can take a course in anything from car maintenance to paper sculpture, from book-binding to yoga, or cordon bleu cookery to fly-fishing.

All you need to do to join is write to us at the National Federation of Women's Institutes, 104 New Kings Road, London SW6 4LY, or telephone 0171 371 9300, and we will put you in touch with WIs in your immediate locality. We hope to hear from you.

THANK YOU, WI

"FIVE years have whizzed by since my husband and I bought our farm, perched high on its Welsh hillside looking down the valley to the sea and the distant winter-white mountains of Snowdonia. As we were totally new to the area I decided to join the WI, primarily in search of friendship. This I found in abundance, both in my village's Institute and, unexpectedly and rapidly, throughout the Federation.

On joining, my initial reaction was one of admiration (and to be honest, some degree of trepidation) at so much remarkable talent among the 27 members. Was I going to be useless? My only skills were midwifery to sheep and singing in the bath but an unimagined variation of activities within the WI unfolded, and everyone's enthusiasm was so infectious. To my amazement I quickly became involved. I found skills I had never tried before, and some which, previously, I had not considered of any value. What a splendid widening of horizons WI has given and how rewarding the socializing together is, compared with the present day tendency towards passive entertainment, each in one's own home glued to the TV.

I have found myself helping to decorate carnival floats, playing in our own WI Federation League darts matches in local pubs, joining the Federation choir, and being one of the team taking our Institute's co-operative exhibit to represent Dyfed-Ceredigion at the 1993 Royal Welsh Show. I have been to Denman College on a Stick Dressing course, a great experience, which led to my name going on the Federation's Combined Arts subcommittee. I've even become very competent at driving backwards. Though never winners at car treasure hunts, we do have hilarious fun. It's the working together as a team that is the real cement of companionship.

As an Institute we have cooked for our Annual St David's Day Cawl Supper, and catered (don't we all!) for village events, parties, shows and, sadly, funerals. With Federation we have been orienteering, canoeing and play reading; competed in rallies; visited theatres, factories and eisteddfodau; attended resolutions meetings, carol services, AGMs, pantomime workshops, International Evenings, Strawberry Fair and duck races, and a great many more events.

All this is extra to our own Institute's weekly meetings. Of these, one per month is for 'business matters', with different members devising their own 'social time' afterwards. The rest are filled with variety, from wild-life slides to country dancing; trying a craft; walks and a meal (husbands too), beetle drives, making our own live magazine, fun auctions, recipe tastings, ghost stories and quizzes. Most enjoyable, too, are meetings such as 'Any Questions', or a Hallowe'en Party when we invite neighbouring Institutes to join us, or vice versa. We have packed parcels for Bosnia and given the village a spring clean and our team of scarecrows in Cardigan town's (12 miles away) pancake races only lost to the police (with young men!).

Holiday-makers to this beautiful and quiet region often ask, 'But what do you do in the winter?' We tell them about the WI, often surprising them with its true 1990s' image. I am so grateful for this happy life. *Diolch yn fawr Sefydliad y Merched* – Thank you very much, Women's Institute – yes, our Federation has classes for learning Welsh too!

Cerith Olerenshaw,
Wig and District WI, Dyfed-Ceredigion.

Denman College, seen from across the lake in winter.

INTRODUCTION

THE WI is a British institution, as much a part of the countryside as green fields and cow parsley. Every village with signs of a caring hand has a WI just as it once had an assured village shop and a church with its own unshared parson. The largest national voluntary organization for women, at village level it may project an image both mild and cosy, yet a young journalist attending a conference on a national issue at which the National Federation of WIs was giving evidence heard a murmur in her ear from a distinguished male colleague, 'You want to watch this lot. They're power.'

'...you want to watch this lot. They're power...'

A Women's Institute, which is what the WI stands for, may be as small as 15 members or as large as 150, though the average is likely to be around 40. Meeting once a month, you might think they are small beer, yet there are nearly 9,000 of these meetings, on various days of the week and at different times of the day, in England, Wales and the off-shore islands.

Around 300,000 women make up the National Federation, more members than the great majority of trade unions. For the record, some 3,000 delegates and members attend its Intermediate General Meetings. At its Triennial General Meetings the number of delegates and members actually attending under its democratic constitution rises to almost 10,000, making this by far and away the largest general meeting of any national organization in the United Kingdom.

But it is not a trade union, although it supports the advancement of women's rights. It speaks up as strongly for children, health issues and the protection of the environment. Over the years its firm, informed voice has been raised on a wide variety of social issues. Never strident, never aggressive, it carries its point by the common sense of its approach and the solid background of factual homework which goes into the presentation of each case.

The National Federation of Women's Institutes is not a pressure group: it owes allegiance to no political party, subscribes to no particular religion and is open to all women – and girls – with no top limit! What all have in common is a sense of belonging, a joy in companionship, in sharing skills and pursuing knowledge and in enjoying themselves. Women working together and sharing each other's company in a range of activities have a great fund of laughter with which to leaven the daily round.

'...no particular party ... no particular religion ... open to all women...'

9

The WI member is married, single, divorced, separated, widowed, living with a partner. She is housewife, student, secretary, scientist, gardener, chef, shopkeeper, craftswoman, doctor, teacher, manager, journalist, writer, artist, poet, singer, actress, lecturer, cleaner, driver, mechanic, pilot; any woman anywhere. Usually, however, she is in close contact with country life, caring about her surroundings and her community. She may just be starting adult life, be a young mother or a granny, be working, retired or unemployed; there's a place for everyone.

'...there's a place for everyone...'

In the WI of today there are Institutes whose members are mainly retired, living in villages whose populations remain little changed. There are others where there are new housing estates and morning meetings with a creche for the toddlers. Evening meetings suit the working woman; there are even lunchtime sessions where that is the most convenient time. When new WIs are formed, adaptability is the name of the game for the Voluntary County Organizers. The only members empowered to form or disband WIs, they are nationally appointed, and trained to recognize the needs of others and to work out ways of accommodating those needs.

Young women join to get away from their children and housework for a while, to meet other people and 'talk about something else'. Older women may join when they retire, to keep their minds active and mix with people from different backgrounds. All stay because their WI is a fund of news and information; new developments in their area, who's moved, died, had a baby, bought a microwave. But, more importantly, they hear about and discuss the wider news of the day, which may have come to them from their County Federation or from the National Executive; a government Green Paper, for example, inviting comment; planning proposals or pending legislation that could affect their future lives. Their discussions are based on shared interests and are pursued in an atmosphere completely free from outside pressure. When it is 'just friends', everyone joins in.

This kind of environment encourages confidence. 'When I saw the women on the platform talking so confidently and well I was absolutely terrified. I thought "I'll never do that", but four years later, there I was, doing it myself.' Set up to make rural life bearable, to educate rural women in order to raise the standards of family life and childcare, the WI has become one of the guardians of the countryside and country living, and also a potent educational force, forward-looking and innovative.

'...guardians of the countryside and country living, and a potent educational force, forward-looking and innovative...'

Through the WI, women can advance themselves if they wish to gain experience in public life, or acquire organizational and management skills that are vocationally recognized. Through the WI, skills can be learned, measured and tested. Standards of excellence in innumerable crafts are notably formidable. The WI has commissioned musical works and staged drama festivals and craft exhibitions on a national scale. In the WI a woman can learn skills in her own village, find classes, competitions and day-schools in her own county, or attend a course at her own residential college. Denman College ran 565 courses in 1994, and now welcomes more than 6,000 students a year.

Most people know the WI through their local market – a shop window for the side of WI life that deals in domestic economy. But if you find those market stalls endearingly artless, consider that no less than 550 markets achieved an annual national turnover in 1993 of £10.5 million. WI Markets operates as a separate body since the WI, being a charity, is not allowed to trade for profit.

The WI also has a publishing arm which, for similar reasons, has been professionalized. Books on a variety of subjects have been produced for many years. WI Books came into being to meet the demands of a membership endlessly voracious for new things to learn or do, and new and better ways of doing them.

But what about that membership? Can anyone join or is it just for countrywomen? Well, mainly; though, as in most walks of present-day life, things are not quite what they used to be. Until 1965 WIs could only be formed in communities where the number of inhabitants did not exceed 4000. That meant, as was the original intention, country villages.

Now the '4000' rule has gone. Villages which had populations of less than four thousand when they formed a WI grew bigger. Try taking their WI away from them! And a new clamour to join was coming from small towns and even the outer suburbs of cities. Richmond and its Hill may be part of London suburbia for most of us, but its famous Lass has her WI. New WIs spring up wherever the need makes itself felt and Federation rules can be met. Conversely, some long-established WIs close as their membership grows old and numbers fall below the level of viability. The majority of members still devote a goodly chunk of their time to rural life, especially as the WI involves not only women but, very often, their families as well.

A young male colleague once complained to me that men, too, needed something like the WI but had not got it. 'We need friends, and safe space too. We've nowhere to go for that kind of support.' Yes, WI members are sociable; they like to meet other people. They care, too, about their families, their friends, their communities and their environment. They support one another. They work hard for themselves and everything they feel strongly about.

By and large they do not complain, they aspire; they want to do things better. Most are creative in one form or another. Most are home-makers. They like to learn, to find out about things, to know what is going on. If they do not like something they want to be able to say so, to have a chance to change it. They do not pass by on the other side.

Today they are energetic and active; games, sports, walking, climbing, swimming, they do it all, and travel too, at home and abroad. If they have reached the stage at which they sit and watch, well, it's because they have probably done it all before. They really enjoy organizing things. Their WIs are financially self-supporting, and ingenious in finding ways of paying their way. They are generous to the less fortunate, as they have always been, and work willingly to support day centres, the disabled, the poor, the distressed and the hungry.

'...all were passionate in their defence of the countryside...'

1: ROOTS AND BRANCHES 1915–1939

WHEN we talk about the beginnings of the WI movement we are also talking about the state of rural Britain. Yet any account of the WI must look at the present as well as the past. Today is where we make tomorrow's history. For some contemporary WI members the old values remain little disturbed. The traditional tasks continue. Lambing, ploughing and harvesting, though transformed by science and technology, are still the daily background to many monthly WI meetings.

Yet rural life itself has changed. Many a country lane has become a highway, many a high street a major trunk road. Many a village is a deafening and dangerous throughway for heavy goods traffic carrying produce from one end of the world to the other, making nonsense of the old seasons when strawberries, for example, were the very symbol of the English midsummer.

To buy the basic necessities of life we increasingly shop at the nearest supermarket, and that, of course, will be in the nearest town. Nor does it stop there. Schools, post offices, even pubs, have joined in the great migration from small to less small and from less small to large. A growing number of WI members find themselves forced to treat Little Magnum cum Parva as a pleasant outpost of the nearest conurbation, with local gossip all too easily swamped by what pours, morning noon and night, from the local city-based radio station.

The green and pleasant spaces of England and Wales offer enjoyable compensation for the stresses imposed upon the family whose daily bread is earned in town or city. They increasingly live a semi-urban life in rural surroundings. The WI, in the latest of many changes from its original rôle, has a vital part to play in adapting to this new mix of town and country and in showing newcomers that there is more to life than the pale and untypical imitations they may see of it on the television screen. 'You know, in the old days we all knew each other but minded our own business,' said one old man. 'Now we all know each other's business but don't know each other.'

It is a far cry from the villages in which the WI began and still thrives. And it's even farther from the reasons and purposes for which the movement came into being.

When Britain became an industrial nation, the new factories produced vast quantities of goods for sale both at home and in overseas markets.

Other countries paid for our manufactured goods with raw materials that included grain, meat and fruit, undercutting British farmers.

The resulting slump in home agriculture, together with the appalling standards of working life in rural areas, brought about a flood of labour from country to town and from fields to factories. Increasing dependence on imported foodstuffs alarmed both landowners and parliament and in 1901 the government set up the Agricultural Organization Society to examine ways in which rural life might be improved and agriculture revived.

'...a movement destined to embrace the globe came from the bereavement of one particular mother...'

In Canada rural isolation was the norm and it was there that the catalyst leading to the founding of a movement destined to embrace the globe came from the death of one particular child, or, rather, from the bereavement of one particular mother. Adelaide Hoodless lived a farming life in Ontario. The loss of her fourth child led her to promote the education of rural women in the fundamentals of hygiene and child care.

She called for women to have the same opportunity as men to get together to learn from and help each other and to seek expert outside knowledge in order to improve life for themselves and their families. From her initiative, Women's Institutes came into being on 19 February, 1897, in Stoney Creek, Ontario. Adelaide Hoodless went on to campaign for women's education and the WI spread like wildfire across Canada.

'...no higher vocation has been given to women than that of home-maker and citizen builder...'

Not only women were WI enthusiasts. By 1911 the movement had gained the recognition of the Canadian government. 'No higher vocation has been given to women than that of home-maker and citizen builder,' said Mrs Hoodless, and her maxim that 'A nation cannot rise above the level of its homes' is as true today as it ever was.

By 1915 the German blockade of allied shipping was already affecting the nation's food supplies. In that year alone there were more than 500,000 British casualties and increasing numbers of women were leaving the land to serve the industrial war effort. The effect upon rural life in general, and the countrywoman in particular, may be imagined.

'...rural women in Britain were second-class citizens in a disintegrating world...'

In 1915 rural women in Britain were second-class citizens in a disintegrating world; no vote, educationally deprived, living, for the most part, lonely lives in dreary, insanitary conditions and losing their menfolk to a brutal war.

Mrs Alfred Watt, an organizer of the Canadian Women's Institute movement and widowed, came to England with her son. Invited to

The first members of the first WI in Britain, Llanfairpwll, Anglesey, 1915.

speak at a conference arranged by the Agricultural Organization Society, she talked about the pioneering work of the Women's Institutes in Canada. Mr Nugent Harris, secretary of the AOS, recognized that here was a way to revitalize rural communities from within.

At the invitation of another innovator, Colonel Richard Stapleton-Cotton, a meeting was arranged in his village. That village, hardly more memorable or less easily pronounced, was Llanfairpwllgwyngyllgogerychwyrndrobwllllantysiliogogogoch (known as Llanfairpwll or Llanfair PG) in Anglesey.

The women of Llanfairpwll knew a good thing when they heard of it. In rural Wales there was no place where women could meet that was not dominated by chapel, church or politics. Women certainly never went to the local pub! Those few places where women could meet other women in mixed company were dominated by men, who did all the talking. Women were expected to know their place. Yet at that meeting on 11 September, 1915, when the first WI was formed in these islands, they pledged that their Institute would become 'a centre for good in the village'.

'...the women of Llanfairpwll knew a good thing when they heard of it...'

The AOS appointed Mrs Watt, originally for three months, to organize the formation of Women's Institutes wherever she could throughout England and Wales. The second WI, at Singleton in Sussex, was closely

'...Mrs Watt's enthusiasm fired women to start WIs, and spread their delight in their newly discovered ability and confidence from village to village...'

followed by others; there were 24 in the first year, 137 by 1917. Mrs Madge Watt's inspirational enthusiasm fired women to start WIs, run them unaided, and spread their delight in their newly discovered ability and confidence from village to village. The original spark was hers.

This was a novel, revolutionary movement: whoever had heard of a gathering where servants had equal standing with their mistresses, where estate employees' wives were on the same footing as the lady of the manor? The news travelled up, down and sideways. Queen Mary was intrigued; she met Mrs Watt and the spark worked again. Mrs Watt was invited to Sandringham to talk to the people on the royal estate. The Queen and Princess Mary came to the meeting, not just as gracious presences but to listen and ask questions like everyone else.

How to impress a Queen? 'My talk was in no way different from usual. I spoke of the simplicity, democracy and friendliness of our movement, of the independence of our Womens' Institutes, each being self-governing and self-supporting, and of the sense of responsibility of every member to her institute.'

'...the Queen is an extraordinary ordinary member...'

A WI was formed at Sandringham and Queen Mary joined. Not surprisingly, she became president, if not a regular taker of the chair. The custom has continued. The Queen Mother is still president of Sandringham WI and the Queen is an extraordinary ordinary member, as are some other members of the family in their respective villages.

The first programme of an organization set up to 'improve the conditions of rural life' concentrated on hygiene, home economy, rabbit breeding, fruit and vegetable preserving, all of them reflecting the then state of village and farm practices.

'...an explosion of mental awakening...'

But around the tables the talk ranged widely; these were not women who had come together solely to 'do good' for the country. They were out to achieve an improvement in themselves, to learn something about the world, to open their minds to subjects they had never had the opportunity to consider before. It was an explosion of mental awakening which would have an immense and highly reactive fallout.

Mrs Watt continued to work for two years for the Agricultural Organization Society, but in 1917 they handed over the growing responsibility to the Board of Agriculture. The Board looked around for someone else to carry on the good work. They needed a figurehead. The qualifications were easy to list, difficult to meet: someone eminent but also capable, sufficiently empathetic and experienced to deal at one and the same time with unsophisticated countrywomen and government departments.

The right person would have to know sufficient about procedure to be able to draw up a constitution and rules, run meetings and, equally important, find people suitable and willing to serve on the committees.

They had the good fortune to hit upon Lady Denman. As the wife of the Governor-General of Australia she was certainly eminent. Daughter of a brilliant engineer and, later, press magnate, she inherited from him an incisive mind, reforming zeal and absolute honesty. He also ensured that she should have a sound and independent financial base from which to contribute actively to public life.

Other advantages were her age, 33, and boundless energy. In Australia she had been actively involved in the welfare of countrywomen. In England she had served on the committee of the feminine arm of what in those days was a formidable Liberal Party. Here she learned committee procedure and political skills at the side of able practitioners.

A pruning test for WI members taking practical courses in Agriculture (1918). In wartime, every traditional masculine task was taken over by women.

Lady Denman took over the WI with enthusiasm, dedicating herself to making it an organization that could withstand stress, strain and – significantly – outside influences. In this she notably succeeded. At a

general meeting of the existing County Federations – in the same month as the October Revolution in Russia – the National Federation of Women's Institutes (NFWI) was born. At first grant-aided by the Board of Agriculture, by 1919 the NFWI was self-governing.

For thirty years Lady Denman was the WI. Appointed at first to direct, she swiftly created a democratic structure. Election to office was through written nomination and secret ballot by members, to ensure complete confidentiality at every level from WI through County to National Federation. She herself duly stood, and was elected, year by year, for the rest of her thirty-year term of office.

The first WIs, 137 in number by the time of the first general meeting, did not start off knowing everything; they worked things out as they went along. Certain principles, however, were clear and shining; an organization, 'open to all women whatever their politics or religion, that would work for the improvement of rural life through the education of countrywomen and was based on the spiritual ideals of fellowship, truth, tolerance and justice'.

'...based on the spiritual ideals of fellowship, truth, tolerance and justice...'

The only qualificaton to the aims originally promoted by Lady Denman was introduced by a subsequent chairman of the Federation, Lady Albemarle. Briefly removing a velvet glove to reveal an iron fist she said, 'The history of the movement is one of intolerance', and went on to list a great many things the NFWI was dedicated to changing over the course of time. Many of those social evils and injustices to which she referred have since been eliminated but the WI's enlightened intolerance is never short of new targets.

'...the WI's enlightened intolerance is never short of new targets...'

Lady Denman looked for others to join her, and in Grace Hadow she found a partner to complement her own talents. Grace Hadow became her vice-chairman. Although a don and an intellectual she nevertheless had the rare gift of understanding simple needs and aspirations.

Writing in those early years she referred to countrywomen 'meeting once a month to discuss matters of interest to them all. Nothing could sound simpler', yet 'nothing could be more significant of the change that has permeated to remote hamlets ... As a nation we are beginning to think for ourselves ... We go about with a perpetual "Why?" in our minds if not on our lips.' On the answer to that "Why?", she continued, depended the fate of our country, 'for it involves the meaning of democracy'.

'...as a nation we are beginning to think for ourselves...'

Lady Denman was the expert on procedure and set a standard of committee work and meeting management which was masterly. Handed down through succeeding leaders of the movement, it has made the

NFWI a model of smooth efficiency which impresses visitors to Federation or National meetings. The Welsh Federations' 1994 annual meeting was programmed to finish with 'three minutes in hand', and without hassle or hustle, it did just that.

Grace Hadow encouraged a leavening of culture among the handicraft and horticultural interests of members: the spirit had to grow in well-being as well as the body.

On the financial side the new National Federation was also fortunate in having Mrs Helena Auerbach, treasurer of the National Union of Women's Suffrage up to 1917, who was able to place the monetary affairs of the growing organization on a firm footing.

The original membership subscription was 2 shillings a year at a time when the average agricultural wage was 46 shillings a week and a girl in living-in domestic service was paid, in addition to her keep, the magnificent sum of 5 shillings a month. Subscriptions alone could not meet the expenses of the movement, even when so much of the work was voluntary. The grant from the Agricultural Development Fund continued, but independence also meant standing on their own financial feet. An endowment fund was set up with the help of £5,000 from Lady Denman, on the understanding that the WIs themselves would match it by their own efforts. This they did.

Trips and outings helped to enlarge the horizons of the village-bound WI women in the early days. A charabanc outing in 1921.

Federations too raised their own funds, and less and less of the government grant was needed to help them. Membership, and consequently contributions, gradually increased: in 1927, twelve years after the founding of the first WI, government assistance was dispensed with altogether.

But countrywomen were not concerned solely with setting up their own network. They had lived through a terrible war. By the 1918 armistice three quarters of a million men had been killed, with another million and a half permanently disabled. The army that remained was of women widowed, sonless, or single and likely to remain so. They too were having to stand on their own feet and manage their own affairs.

Throughout the war women had played their full part, working on the land and in the factories, running their homes and rearing their children, often unaided. They had scrimped and managed, nursed and suffered. Now that peace had come they were determined to achieve an improvement in their lives and environment. They knew that life could be better and they set out to make themselves heard.

'...they knew that life could be better and they set out to make themselves heard...'

When training 'her' organizers Mrs Watt had urged them to 'improve the conditions of rural life by stimulating interest in the agricultural industry, by developing co-operative enterprises, by encouraging home and local industries, by the study of home economics and by providing a centre for educational and social intercourse and for all local activities.'

Developing co-operative enterprises included selling the surplus crops of increasingly productive gardens and smallholdings. Produce markets, started informally in Criccieth, then, more systematically, in Lewes, began their steady progress towards recognition and independence.

Federations and the NFWI alike set about house hunting. In many cases starting from a corner of the local National Farmers' Union offices, a marathon of money-raising began to fund premises for Federation houses and a London headquarters. Lady Denman bought a house in Eccleston Street, Victoria, and leased it to the WI. With a powerbase at last, targets were set and met. A house enables staff to have desks and a telephone, to provide 'a centre for educational and social intercourse' and to be the venue for all committee meetings and conferences. In addition it provides an address from which information can be disseminated and to which it can come.

'...a centre for educational and social intercourse...'

Federation houses are often more than offices: they provide teaching centres, central meeting places and social venues for members, as well as depositaries for such things as drama wardrobes and exhibition stands.

WIs in their villages socialized, studied, practised their traditional skills and learned new ones, the most useful of which was how to organize, express their opinions and make them heard. Resolutions were put to Federation and National meetings on subjects as diverse as women jurors, agricultural wages, adult education, protection for birds, food hygiene and the humane slaughter of animals.

Concentrated in rural areas because of the rule that 'a WI may only be formed in places with a population of less than 4000', the movement still thrived to such an extent that women on the outskirts of towns applied to join their nearest villages.

The WIs put themselves on the map. For one thing they showed their work. The first national event was a craft exhibition in 1917. Queen Mary attended and the affair was widely reported. Standards were being set and the WI began to establish its reputation for excellence; only the best was chosen for display and competition was intense.

'...the WI began to establish its reputation for excellence...'

Normal expectation then was that women who married ceased any paid employment and stayed at home to keep house and rear children. There were many women with active brains and time on their hands. They did not set out to change the world overnight but, recognizing that the world could do with change, they chipped away at it bit by bit.

It was vital that the organization should maintain its independence from outside interests if it were to achieve the confidence to manage its own affairs. It could not allow itself to be taken over by squirearchy, political parties or, most notably in Wales where church and chapel ruled most aspects of rural life, organized religion.

Queen Mary at the (1917) National Crafts Exhibition in Hyde Park.

Needless to say, there were teething troubles, not least in establishing the delicate balance between the Federations, already up and running before the National Federation drew them together, the National Executive Committee, which had to devise rules and procedures acceptable to the movement as a whole, and the Voluntary County Organizers (VCOs).

Organizers, originally appointed by the then Board of Agriculture, dressed in a uniform – in wartime, uniform of any kind was covetable – of brown corduroy suits and 'sensible' hats, were personally appointed, trained and inspired by Mrs Watt. Organizers became voluntary when the National Federation achieved its own independence. Chosen by their Federations, they were trained and appointed, as they still are, by the National Federation.

'...VCOs personally appointed, trained and inspired by Mrs Watt...'

To ensure involvement at all levels a Consultative Council was set up. Elected representatives of each Federation were to meet with the National Executive to confer with and advise the NFWI and keep it informed on members' points of view. Council met twice a year, once in London to select the resolutions that would be debated at the Annual General Meeting, and once, to increase participation, in another part of the country. VCOs were invited as observers. They were there to watch the process, not to make decisions. Decision-making was the job of those elected for that purpose.

The Press took note of the movement's growing competence. In 1930, when the AGM was held in Blackpool, the West Lancashire Evening Gazette made a typical comment, many times echoed since: 'The 3,000 women at the conference of the WI have come for business, there is no doubt about that. They are punctual, systematic, rigorously obedient to the rules of debate; one had only to see them at the conference to discover how much they could teach many a male congress that thinks it knows all about running an affair like this.'

'...the WI have come for business, there is no doubt about that. They are punctual, systematic, rigorously obedient to the rules of debate...'

Jerusalem, the battle hymn of campaigning reformers, was chosen as the WI 'anthem' only after WIs were invited to write a suitable song for themselves. Since one of the submissions began, 'We are a band of earnest women', one should be grateful that William Blake won the day. Why 'Jerusalem'? A recent item in the Leicester and Rutland newsletter answered the question. How was it, asked editor Stella Elliot, that the WI anthem is 'a poem by a half-mad visionary who used to wander about the countryside muttering to himself?'

'A burning desire for change can work miracles,' she concluded, 'and we can create Jerusalem ... The WI is a bit short of bows, spears, and arrows of burning gold or otherwise. We are commonly supposed to

Northcourt WI choir, 1927. Singing flourishes in small communities like this one.

wield jam spoons. So the next time we sing "I shall not cease from mental fight, nor shall my sword sleep in my hand" (and whether our particular sword is a jam spoon, a typewriter or a set of secretary's minutes) remember that, like Blake, we're just trying to make the world a little bit better.'

The reputation of the WI grew and spread: its effectiveness as a catalyst for beneficial change was also noted in high places.

In 1931, in answer to a plea for help from Tregaron, Cardiganshire, surgeon Mr William Evans of the cardiac unit of the London Hospital referred to 'the black picture you had to paint' in the matter of death statistics in maternal and child welfare. He advised that 'to flourish, the energy (to achieve improvement) must come from within the locality.' Nearby villages, he said, had their Women's Institutes. 'There should be one started in Tregaron this coming winter, for herein lies the secret of extending to rural areas facilities that would otherwise be unavailable.

'*...to flourish, the energy (to achieve improvement) must come from within the locality...*'

'There is only one way of fitting women for the work of raising standards of nurture and hygiene and that is through the energy of the

Women's Institutes. The secret of success lies with the womenfolk of Tregaron and their ability to sink sect and creed and strive in union for the noble cause that must bring benefit to the whole community.' His words were promptly acted upon. The Tregaron WI came into being to make its contribution, along with its sister WIs, to all the 'noble causes' to which the movement is dedicated.

In the meantime, though executive committees may have dealt with the minutiae of policy and procedure in the National Federation, in the villages they just got on with it.

'...strive in union for the noble cause that must bring benefit to the whole community...'

Lady Denman, with her usual honesty, said, 'There have been moments when I thought that Miss Hadow and I must have been distinctly bright because our Women's Institutes have gone so well. Fortunately I have realized that the Institutes just flourish by themselves and that even in counties where the leaders are incredibly stupid they still survive.'

'... the WI was the place to be and girls couldn't wait to be old enough to join, it was the only thing in the village...'

They were 'centres for good' as Llanfairpwll had vowed; they were dynamos of energy as Mr William Evans had observed; it was 'the place to be and girls couldn't wait to be old enough to join, it was the only thing in the village' and it did 'improve the conditions of rural life'. In fact, they revitalised it. The WIs formed drama groups and choirs, went on outings and exchanged books. They expressed their gratitude to the Carnegie Trust for making rural libraries possible. Some wrote poetry, some made quilts; they were busy, busy, busy. But they had time to worry constructively too.

When they felt strongly about something, they got support from everyone. Kelmscott WI was the first to call for hot meals for school-children, Langton Matravers initiated protection for wild birds and Girton WI roused opinion against the use of fur from trapped animals. In 1927 the Isle of Wight Federation pointed out the dangers of marine pollution and Colesbourne WI became alarmed at the destruction of wild flowers.

'...all were passionate in their defence of the countryside while fighting to make life in it more comfortable...'

All were passionate in their defence of the countryside while fighting to make life in it more comfortable. But industrial depression led to new poverty, strikes and unrest. On the continent the rise of fascism in Italy and Germany sent quivers of alarm through the nervous system of the western world.

During the First World War the WIs were enlisted in the struggle to increase food production in the face of the threat from German U-boats. As another conflict loomed, the threat from German under-sea warfare promised to be larger than ever.

2: EYES FRONT, BEST FOOT FORWARD 1939–1945

WHERE did the WI stand in the event of war? This was what National Executive and members asked themselves. Lady Denman, who was also to assume responsibility for the formation and deployment of the Women's Land Army, had no doubts.

In June 1938 National Executive circulated all WIs advising them that although they could give valuable help by arranging for hospitality for evacuated mothers and children, and by assisting as good neighbours in home safety services, they should not directly involve themselves as a movement in such things as air raid precautions. This, ran the directive, was the responsibility of the local authorities and concerned all citizens equally.

The Executive was concerned to preserve the non-sectarian nature of the movement and, in particular, to respect the beliefs of its Quaker members. All the same, the ruling caused a good deal of controversy. Some members felt they should, as a body, help the war effort in any way possible. Lady Denman remained adamant, pointing out that there was nothing to stop members supporting the war effort as individuals.

And of course they did. Many of the younger women went into uniform and left for the Services or the Land Army. Others met the insatiable need for female labour in the armaments industry. But in general, tens of thousands of WI members, especially older women and

'...in this great struggle we are keyed up to a higher level, we have more vision, more faith...' Home and Country

Left to right: Florence Lilley, Florence Hewitt, Dalton Mackay Brown, Nellie Bradley, May Horsford, inspecting the red currant crop at the wartime Jam Centre in 1940. Dean WI, Bedfordshire. The WI made the baskets too.

'A tea break for the canners.'
Sharing labour, sharing jokes –
lightens the load.

young mothers, not only responded to the intensive drive for increased agricultural production by working the farms but gave invaluable help wherever and in whatever form it was needed.

A new Women's Voluntary Service was set up by the Home Secretary, specifically to enrol volunteers for a variety of community services. Many WI members independently became ARP wardens, firewatchers or joined such services as the Red Cross and the St John's Ambulance Brigade.

At government request the National Federation drew up detailed plans for the evacuation of mothers and children from cities under the imminent threat of bombing. When evacuation did come it was the WVS that organized it but it was to the villages and mainly to the WI that the children went. The WI as a movement refused to allow itself to be sidelined by its National Executive in its wartime contribution. Its members simply fought the war on different fronts, concentrating, as always, on what they had always done best.

The enemy was 'waste, want and woe', a frontline effort so far as the civilian population was concerned. More to the point, in a war where each side counted on breaking the other's morale, the WI kept their meetings going.

'Volunteers were asked to work on the land,' recounts West Bergholt WI. 'A War Savings group was formed; there were house-to-house collections of rags and bones for the government; cotton reels were collected, and surplus vegetables sold to the Navy. Members helped at the preservation centres where jams and pickles were made; various government sponsored weeks were held: the Spitfire Fund; Warships Week; Salute the Soldier Week. The WI ran whist drives and donated the proceeds. Books and toys were sent to the Prisoner of War Children's Fund.' They don't mention that the NFWI as a body collected enough money to present three ambulances to the medical services.

WIs in the First World War had learned how to produce and use everything edible. This time they had an organisation behind them and good communication. Once again they set about stocking the national larder. Nor was it confined to the obvious crops. There is food value in hedgerow blackberries and moorland bilberries. In the almost total absence of imported fruit other than concentrated orange juice, alternative sources of all-important vitamins had to be exploited. Even the 'roses round the door' could produce rosehip syrup.

Wartime jam production is not just a story but a veritable saga, even today worth the retelling. Conscious of the need to preserve everything that could be used to supplement the national larder, the National Federation bought and distributed to the counties £1400 worth – a mighty sum by present day standards – of sugar for preserving.

'...one ton of mixed rags makes 250 battle dresses and 30 Army tents; 300,000 tons of kitchen waste maintains 15,000 pigs; 6 old bills make a washer for a shell; one envelope makes 50 cartridge wads...' Home and Country

'...this time they had an organisation behind them and good communication...'

School for Produce Guild Leaders. Digging for victory. Every yard and every acre became productive (1942)

This fruit was preserved with government issue sugar and went into the shops on ration.

They also bought some canners. These hand-operated sealing machines were something new to the WI but necessary if the traditional jar was to be supplemented by sturdy, longlife storage. The women quickly learned how to use them and teams went from village to village, efficiently canning what their sister WIs had gathered in. By the end of 1940 the WIs had picked, bottled and canned 1630 tons – over three and a half million pounds – of fruit and vegetables. As the war progressed, so did the figure rise.

Nationally there was neither labour to spare for fruit picking nor petrol to get it all to jam factories. The preserving centres set up in village halls, garden sheds, individual kitchens or in mobile canning vans sent from America did a sterling job: the recognition of the quality of the jams by the House of Commons in the great jam war of 1981 was no more than belated commendation for a heroic as well as hot and sticky campaign. The women fought on the jam front with pans, spoons, weighing scales and sheer 'stickability', and all was sent to the national larder. So far as the WI was concerned there had been jam yesterday and there would be jam today and tomorrow. They kept none for themselves, in spite of preserving vast quantities of fruit for the nation.

'...the women fought on the jam front with pans, spoons, weighing scales and sheer stickability...'

In Hawkinge WI in East Kent, just five members remained. Yet, in that summer of 1940, alone and unaided they jammed, bottled or canned their own harvest and those from the plots of all the vacated houses. Hawkinge RAF station was itself the target of repeated attacks. Spitfires and Hurricanes of Fighter Command scrawled the contrails of a hot and sunny September over their heads, locked in battle with the Luftwaffe. The five worked on in a farm kitchen.

They made and canned 784 pounds of jam in the torrid heat of sun and cooker, often all but stripped to the waist according to one of them. Of all the WIs that made preserves these Hawkinge women made the third highest total. The contemporary President of Hawkinge reports that for many years they had a fund that was held separately from the normal WI money, called 'the Jam money'. 'It was the profit made over the war years for WI funds,' she said, 'but no one could bear to spend it, although we've put it in the deposit account now.'

All around the country the story was the same. Those WI members left at home sewed, cooked, knitted, 'made do' and mended. They not only bred rabits to feed their family and friends; they cured their skins and made fur coats for Russia. They sent food parcels for the crews of mine-sweepers, for prisoners of war, ran canteens for the troops, opened their homes to servicemen and women far from their own families.

The times could hardly have been grimmer but many present-day members knew the other side. They were young, history was being made, and in spite of the sacrifice and seemingly endless set-backs there was excitement. They could not go abroad, unless it was in support of the troops, but 'abroad' came to them from the four corners of the earth.

'...every person who spreads an atmosphere of cheerfulness and quiet resolution is helping to win the war...' Lady Denman

The jam was taken from the hall to the local grocer's shop by WI jam-making members. Thornton-le-Dale, Yorkshire, 1942.

The author, in wartime uniform.

'... the services which women can give — both as householders looking after children from the larger areas in their own homes and in the thousand and one community tasks — must rank as national service of the first importance...'
Minister of Health

Young men from all over the Empire and half the countries of Europe, as well as hundreds of thousands of American boys, introduced the village girls to new music, new kinds of food and not infrequently a new life. Village populations swelled with soldiers and airmen billeted in cottages; local airfields or anti-aircraft batteries provided partners at the village hops, audiences for concerts, custom for the local pub. WI meetings closed with mottoes from time to time: 'Make good, do good, be good', or 'Wondrous is the gift of cheerfulness'.

The older women had perhaps the hardest time. Deprived of husbands, sons and daughters whom they might never see again, forced to pinch and scrape on food rations that fell steadily and would shock all but the most poverty-stricken today, they ran their homes with literally no help, human or mechanical. As often as they managed to strike a balance, new deprivations were announced. 'In this great struggle,' wrote a contributor to *Home and Country* at the time, 'we are keyed up to a higher level, we have more vision, more faith.'

They needed all this and more with the coming of the evacuees. It was a salutary experience both for town and country. Most of the children came from overcrowded city streets, often from homes even less affluent than those of their rural hostesses.

One half of the nation knew virtually nothing about the other. Before the expected invasion the villages were apprehensive. Their rural inferiority complex made them expect their 'sophisticated' city guests would be altogether smarter, mentally as well as in dress.

The reality was different. The more affluent city-dwellers took care of themselves, like often as not finding like. It was the poor and deprived of the cities, arriving like aliens among country folk who were in many ways deprived themselves, who caused the greatest shock. Some evacuated families were relatively sophisticated, well-informed, and used to a life with modern conveniences. Others, the product of inner-city working-class neglect, were most definitely not.

Three months after the 'invasion' NFWI Executive asked for a survey to report on the condition of the mothers and children as they arrived. Its purpose was 'to determine the social conditions and health education of the community' for the benefit of the authorities. The Executive, already apprehensive of what might be said, stressed that it 'should not be taken in a spirit of grievance but as a definite contribution to the welfare of our fellow citizens'.

The replies were blunt, critical of a national education system which in so many cases had failed to fit young women for family life. Yet they

Miss Rotherham using a canner that was a gift from America; teams went round the villages canning the produce brought in by the WI.

looked on the positive side. As one Welsh WI wrote: 'They were most likeable and well-behaved children. Nearly all of those who were not soon learned to be. After a few weeks they learned to be clean.' They were hard weeks, but they were a shock for city mothers too. Arriving in a world which had never known street lights was one thing. The absence of shops, cinemas, life and bustle was another. The 'townies' had come to houses with very few if any labour-saving gadgets or even, sometimes, indoor sanitation. Some countrywomen had to come to terms with people who were apparently ignorant of simple cooking, basic nutrition, sewing or even personal cleanliness.

Many children were untrained in elementary hygiene. Bedding and mattresses suffered most. Yet many of the mothers fled after the first week; better to face the bombs than the horrors of such primitive living. But a point that seemed to have escaped critics, wrote one enlightened member, 'is that the refugees might themselves be victims.' To exaggerate their deficiencies, she ended, 'does not seem to me to be in accord with the high traditions with which the Women's Institute has always associated itself.'

'...refugees might themselves be victims...'

Sure enough, children, some underfed and ill-clad when they arrived, were soon filling out and settling into a more robust life. Along with

'...Women's Institutes have played a splendid part in the war effort. Whatever the call – billeting, salvage, food production – they have responded whole-heartedly. They will deserve even better of their country if they keep a live faith in its future destiny...'
Winifred Comber

'...women, tipped the balance between victory and defeat...'

'...if you cannot win the war without women, neither can you win the peace...'

their problems they brought a breath of a different kind of fresh air. Perky city kids could play, dance and sing with a repertoire far wider than their country cousins. In return, country children gamely shared their lore and pastimes, teachers organized co-operative activities, and the communities eventually established understanding and mutual respect.

Throughout the war membership of the WI fell steadily But those who were left were already thinking and talking ahead. The intermingling of town and country, the close contacts between villagers and the pick of the world's young men and women as the war in Europe moved towards its final days, could not fail to emphasize what was so obviously lacking and what vision and determination might achieve. And it was the women, with a new independence born of necessity, who did most of the thinking.

Early in 1945 a delegate from the Nottinghamshire Federation reported on a meeting in London of the National Conference of Women, with representatives from all women's organizations. It was called by the government to praise the heroic war work done by women all over the country, to thank them, and to call them to greater effort still. 'Women,' they were told, 'tipped the balance between victory and defeat.'

One of the speakers was Winston Churchill himself, who said, 'No country in the world is better organized than ours. We are ready for any air attack, ready to grow more food, make more munitions, and more ships, care for the sick and wounded and maintain civilian life. This would not be possible but for the women.' Here was an opportunity not to be missed.

Miss Dorothy Elliot, thanking Mr Churchill on behalf of the conference, expressed their gratitude to him 'for taking us into your confidence. You have set the seal on the status of women in the war effort ... But, Sir, you must not, after the war, say that women are too old at 35. We women hate war and we shall find our fullest opportunity for service in the peace, for if you cannot win the war without women, neither can you win the peace.'

Already in 1941 Lady Denman had urged the need for the WI to concern itself with postwar reconstruction. They went further. At the Annual General Meeting delegates were congratulated on a good start towards carrying out postwar responsibilities which included 'the promotion of international understanding, the basis on which the future of the world must be built, the consideration and active presentation of the needs of countrywomen in education, health and housing, the taking by women of a larger share in local government.'

The WIs tackled questionnaires on every aspect of members' lives. Four thousand of them sent in their views on education and the movement was congratulated by the authorities on the practical way in which the evidence was collected and presented. Today such thoroughness as evidenced in the 1993 Report on Carers in Rural Society is everywhere taken as standard for the WI.

To discuss the Education Act of 1944, NFWI held 23 county conferences. The speakers were leading experts and government representatives concerned with the subject under discussion, chaired by a member of the National or Federation Executive.

In 1944, too, an international conference on Freedom from Want was attended not only by NFWI representatives but by foreign guests whose expenses were paid for from NFWI funds. The National Federation had already submitted to the government another memorandum with suggestions for the future of the countryside. A committee was set up, with Lord Justice Scott as chairman, to advise on that very matter.

As Lady Denman was a prominent member of the committee, due weight was given in the final report to matters of close concern to rural communities; good rural housing, women representatives on local authorities, availability of electricity at a cost comparable to that of towns, the provision of water supplies, of village halls and playing fields.

Seated left Doris Cumming, with WI members, gathering an appreciable harvest from the hedgerows.

'...the NFWI had already submitted to the government another memorandum with suggestions for the future of the countryside...'

Lake District National Park. The WI campaigned for safe access to the countryside for town dwellers.

It also recommended the creation of a central planning authority and local planning authorities and, in considering access to the countryside for town dwellers, recommended the setting up of national parks and nature reserves, all subjects of WI resolutions.

At last the WI campaign for the protection of open spaces was having effect, but in recommending the revitalization of country areas the report also commented that 'the cardinal problem is how to refocus cultural life within the village itself'. The NFWI had been working on that objective for twenty years. It had been a growing practice to hold residential conferences of two or three days in various parts of the country, to enable members from different regions to meet. How convenient it would be if they had a suitable venue always available to them.

'...how to refocus cultural life within the village itself...'

The idea was theoretically far beyond the ambitions and abilities of countrywomen many of whom had left school at the age of fourteen. But they were not lacking in vision, confidence in themselves, or faith. The concept of a conference house, the bravest and most adventurous of ideas, was a fitting challenge with which to meet a new era.

3: WEARYING THEM WITH OUR COMING
From resolution to mandate

THINK militant, think WI! Unimaginable? Think again. In 1994 the Alliance of Women's Organizations lobbied Parliament in support of a private member's bill put forward by Harry Cohen MP. The bill proposed a reform of the Law of Provocation, arguing that 'prolonged domestic violence' should be a mitigating factor in the cases of women on trial for taking extreme steps to defend themselves against persistent and cruel marital abuse.

The lobby was mounted by the Alliance of Women's Organizations, of which the NFWI is a member body. Beryl Sutton of Clare WI in Suffolk stirred the WI into active support. As a result NFWI members found themselves demonstrating in company with 500 women representing bodies as diverse as Justice for Women and Southall Black Sisters. An extreme example – in any case, the bill foundered in the parliamentary quagmire after a first reading – but there are undoubtedly times when actions speak louder than words. The WI story is full of them.

'...there are undoubtedly times when actions speak louder than words...'

The WI certainly doesn't 'cease from mental fight' and is sometimes even driven to draw its metaphorical sword. The battle has been fought over a wide range of issues, the front line sometimes encircles the globe, but it is on the home front, by and large, that the most notable victories have been won.

In Llanfairpwll, at the first ever WI meeting, they made their first resolution; it declared quite simply that they 'resolved to be a centre for good in the village'. In 1994 at the Triennial General Meeting, the movement's concern was with laws on obscenity, the donation of organs for transplant, and the restriction of access to legal aid.

'...resolved to be a centre for good in the village...'

Over the course of its 80 years the WI has kept itself informed over a great range of local and national events and made its opinions known to the government of the day. Through its international body, the Associated Countrywomen of the World, it is able to present its views to the United Nations, and through its representation on COFACE (the Confederation of Family Organizations in the European Community) to the European Union.

'...the WI has kept itself informed over a great range of local and national events and made its opinions known to the government of the day...'

There are numerous pathways: they are kept open and weed-free by assiduous cultivation. Every year more than 100 possible resolutions are submitted to the National Federation for discussion at the Annual

Meeting. Even before a resolution gets on to the list it will have been discussed in the proposer's Institute, probably at a Federation meeting, and have been meticulously examined and researched.

Resolutions can be classified quite simply. Priority is given to: rural matters, matters of particular concern to women, matters on which the WI itself can take action. There are resolutions that draw attention to something: drugs, for example, substance abuse, or health issues.

'...resolutions that resolve to do something... and resolutions which urge others to do something...'

There are resolutions that resolve to do something: support day-care centres, for example, help the mentally handicapped, keep Britain tidy, or provide more community care. There are resolutions which urge others to do something: provide better transport or education, for example, give equality of opportunity, protect the environment, or reduce crime.

The Federations hold special meetings, open to all members, at which the shortened list is thoroughly discussed and voted on. They are not voting upon the pros and cons of a particular resolution but on which are worth discussing at all in the sense of offering to the WI and its members an opportunity for action.

When the views of all the Federations have been taken into account, a final list of four or five resolutions is sent back to all WIs. There is time for amendments to be submitted. They must fully discuss and vote on these lists, and instruct a delegate to speak or vote on their behalf at the next Annual or National General Meeting. As General Meetings always take place in June, resolutions are always discussed in May.

'...for one or two months they become encyclopaedic in their knowledge...'

In the merry month of May, through the length and breadth of the land, the same subjects are being gone over with a fine-tooth comb. VCOs, who have all done their even more intensive homework with the help of experts and NFWI briefings, are usually asked to take these meetings and provide background information. For one or two months they become encyclopaedic in their knowledge of donor transplants, the Antarctic, gene engineering or the position of the mentally handicapped in the community. And so do the WIs.

'...this is the tip of an Everest of discussion, the last stage in a very long, very thoroughly explored debate...'

At the General Meeting strangers might be forgiven for thinking that the final resolutions are dealt with far too quickly for serious debate, no matter how good the speakers. They should be reminded that this is the tip of an Everest of discussion, the last stage in a very long, very thoroughly explored debate. Though an individual resolution may have begun its life in some small village meeting, it has travelled far and wide and been put through the kind of grilling a traveller might get when crossing a great many frontiers. If passed, it gets to the final voting stage and becomes a mandate, authorizing the NFWI to take whatever action is required for as long as is necessary: mandates define policy for an indefinite period of time.

Over the decades the range of subjects on which WI members have felt strongly have been wide indeed. In the early years rural matters were dominant; provision of services such as piped, clean water, electricity, waste disposal and health care in a variety of forms. Peace and international understanding were also high on the agenda; the League of Nations up to 1939, the United Nations from the closing stages of the Second World War.

'...over the decades the range of subjects on which WI members have felt strongly have been wide indeed...'

During that war the WI called for reconstruction when peace came, and for food and clothing for refugees in the aftermath. They called for an end to nuclear testing in the days of the Cold War, urged more educational opportunities for women, set up Denman College and addressed a variety of issues in the area of health and hygiene. Child welfare figured on the list, so did equality of opportunity for women in public life.

By the sixties social concerns such as drug taking, violence in print, films and television, and pornography made their appearance. So did wider topics: the protection of the environment, the dangers of certain insecticides, litter and that more dangerous form of litter, pollution.

As the increasing number of mandates clarifies and strengthens WI policy, the fields of action the NFWI is authorized to enter have steadily widened; there are areas in which a mandate has been acted upon so effectively that the original problem no longer exists or an official body has come into being specifically to deal with it. Such mandates can, as it were, be moved onto the back burner while more urgent affairs receive attention.

Sometimes, of course, a mandate needs to be updated or brought back to public attention when there is reason to think it might receive a more sympathetic or effective response. Broadcasting to women in a series of talks, Lady Denman quoted the parable of a woman who went to a judge and laid a complaint before him 'that he might rid me of mine adversary.' But he would not. She went to him yet again. 'Because this woman troubleth me,' he said, 'I will avenge her lest by her continual coming she weary me.' 'Remember this parable,' Lady Denman exhorted her listeners, 'and act accordingly.'

Assertiveness training for women, a growth area in the feminist world in recent years, advocates a 'broken record' technique of constant repetition to wear away opposition. The WI have been using it for a very long time.

'...broken record technique of constant repetition to wear away opposition...'

RESOLUTIONS FROM 1918–1939

The subjects which have led to national mandates reflect the social climate of the time, women's concerns, and the conditions of rural life. They also portray the increasingly wide field of interests in which women have become engaged over the past eighty years.

Rural life and the position of women in society were uppermost in mind from the very beginning. The WI have always been in the forefront in maintaining pressure to protect and preserve the countryside for the benefit of the whole community. They urged equality of opportunity for women to serve in public life as jurors and magistrates, and in the twenties campaigned for women police and probation officers.

The existence of child abuse was recognized and publicized in 1925 and 1930, together with the danger to children from lurid films and publications, a threat returned to in 1961. The WI deplored standards of press reporting and 'lurid pictures' then, as they still do today.

In 1933 and 1943 they urged action in their own communities to help relieve unemployment as 'a social scourge', and undertook to teach crafts at occupational centres for the unemployed in 1934. Education for women in rural areas was pioneered by the WI, and almost annually kept in the spotlight from 1921 onwards.

Colesbourne WI alerted the public to the destruction of wildflowers; the verges blossom.

The dependence on adequate nourishment of the national health led to calls for school meals and milk for children, as well as education in nutrition. Well ahead of its time, the Isle of Wight drew attention to the dangers of marine pollution from ships in 1927. Other resolutions stressed the vital importance of clean water supplies in 1928, 1930, 1934 and as recently as 1993, also the need for the provision of adequate sewage systems in 1937 and 1958, updating the issue in 1970.

It was not only human welfare and happiness that concerned them. Resolutions on cruelty to animals, including safeguarding them from cruel trapping, from ill-treatment in training them to perform, and to prevent the capture and sale of wild birds, were brought in 1921, 1930, 1931, 1933 and 1936. Others opposed the export of horses for food, and urged humane methods of slaughter for livestock reared for domestic consumption.

As part of the conservation of the countryside, Colesbourne WI alerted the public to the destruction of wild flowers, while Langton Matravers called for the protection of wild birds. The campaign against litter, begun in 1925, led to the formation of the Keep Britain Tidy movement and the WI has remained in the vanguard of this battle to the

Clearing up litter as part of the Keep Britain Tidy campaign at Colwinston WI.

present day. They fought for more and better rural housing, sensible planning, adequate postal services and, in 1927, for the provision of rural telephone services, highlighting the isolation of rural communities.

'...highlighting the isolation of rural communities...'

Resolutions to improve agricultural production, education and opportunities for training in agricultural techniques led in 1932 to national support for women's co-operative markets already in operation. WI Markets were helped, initially by the Carnegie Trust, to appoint a markets adviser and develop marketing on a national scale. But the Thirties were a time of tension and growing awareness of the threat of war. Seven resolutions from 1921 onwards supported the League of Nations and urged the active pursuit of peace. In 1927 they recorded the desire to further closer relations with similar organizations of women overseas, reaffirming the work of the Associated Countrywomen of the World, of which the NFWI became a member.

RESOLUTIONS FROM 1939–1945

There were few general meetings during the war; women were preoccupied with the struggle to maintain their homes and with caring for their families and the community. They did find time to emphasize their belief in the equality of the sexes, with a resolution of blunt brevity: that men and women should receive equal pay for equal work. With Toff WI they supported with enthusiasm the ideas in Sir William Beveridge's report on social security, particularly noting that 'health insurance for housewives, and children's allowances are essential if family life is to be free from want', and Courtenhall WI urged that married women and widows 'not gainfully employed' should not be allowed to fall through the insurance net. They urged precedence to be given to efforts to secure 'an ordered opportunity of service and earning for all.' In other words, full employment.

'...an ordered opportunity of service and earning for all...'

In the midst of their own work on the land they recorded their wish to see 'the work of the small producer recognized ... and due provision made for their views, including facilities for organizing, training and marketing.' WI Markets was a major step towards the fulfilment of this aim. Most admirably and bravely, they 'welcomed the suggestion of a Women's Institute college ... and instructed the Executive committee to make the necessary arrangements.' The importance of providing school meals was again given prominence, as was the supply of milk 'at a reasonable price for school cooking'.

Looking ahead, they urged that the provision of village halls should not be forgotten when post-war planners got to grips with reconstruction. In 1943, two years before the end of hostilities, the Essex Federation asked the National Federation of Women's Institutes 'to consider ways and means by which the WI can help in the postwar relief of Europe'.

'...consider ways and means by which the WI can help in the postwar relief of Europe...'

RESOLUTIONS FROM 1945–1969

The WI, reflecting the social concerns of their time, and the prevailing mood of the country, joined West Sussex Federation in pledging support for the emerging United Nations Organization, and continued their co-operation with the Associated Countrywomen of the World. They pressed for consideration to be given to rural health needs in the provision of medical surgeries, dispensing by doctors, availability of vaccination for children, chiropody and dental care for the elderly and more freely available visiting for children in hospital.

Prompted by Essex and Devon Federations and by Threkeld WI in Cumbria, they supported day centres and greater understanding for the mentally handicapped, leading to the formation of 'special WIs' in homes and hospitals for the mentally ill and handicapped, and in some Cheshire Homes.

'...they supported day centres and greater understanding for the mentally handicapped...'

Stapehill WI, Dorset, opposed the easy availability of unsuitable books and comics for children and the increasing amount of violence on film and the now almost universal TV. In 1963 they urged that a new way be found to calculate the domestic rating system and in 1974 just as earnestly demanded the reinstatement of the old one when the alternative proved far from satisfactory. Little did they know what lay in store for them towards the end of the Eighties.

As the permissive age came into being the dangers of drugs and alcohol abuse were thoroughly examined and discussed; if deplored, they were deplored from a background of meticulous research and self-briefing. The WI leaflet on drugs was widely circulated outside the WI.

Always alert to dangers to children, the practice of fostering was examined and supported; maintenance and support for single mothers was urged, and the dangers of fireworks and toxic chemicals in food examined and publicized. The rise in crime and the matter of adequate deterrence came to the fore, as did the inadequacy of housing provision.

With the drastic pruning of the railway system in the name of rationalization, problems of rural transport received a high priority; there were three resolutions and a number of WI initiatives as a result. Post buses came into existence, largely as a result of WI pressure, and still serve the community in many parts of the country. Rural transport has, not surprisingly, continued to be a high priority among the concerns of WI members and is likely to remain so.

Turnstiles in women's public lavatories, a very sore point with women, were vigorously opposed. Backed up by other women's organizations, they have been largely removed: no pregnant woman who has had to struggle through a turnstile would welcome their return.

The provision of clean water and adequate sewage schemes was still on the agenda, as was housing and its provision, particularly for the elderly. In connection with water suplies the WI deplored the flooding of valuable agricultural land to make reservoirs and called for research into desalination. NFWI support for the Freedom from Hunger campaign set off an explosion of activity and a wealth of projects all around the country.

'...the dangers of drugs and alcohol abuse were thoroughly examined ... if deplored, they were deplored from a background of meticulous research and self-briefing...'

'...an explosion of activity and a wealth of projects all around the country...'

Coldharbour, Surrey, gets its post bus.

Coldharbour WI fought long and hard for its post bus. Rene Jackson, Surrey Federation Chairman, WI members and friends welcome the first run.

Increasing concern for the threatened countryside and its conservation led to the establishment of a Town and Country project. Financed by the UK Carnegie Trust, it was taken up by WIs around the country and led in its turn to the This Green and Pleasant Land exhibition which highlighted successful conservation projects north, south, east and west. And aware of far greater, indeed global dangers in a less secure world, the NFWI urged all governments to ban nuclear testing in the atmosphere.

In 1972, twenty-one eight-year olds from a school in one of the more overcrowded and decrepit areas of Westminster spent the day in the Surrey countryside as guests of Abinger Common and Wotton WI as part of the Town and Country Project. A riotous time was had by all. Eileen O'Kelly and Daphne Cox presided over the barbecue while an assortment of WI daughters, husbands, friends and an even larger assortment of wellies collected from all over the village, ensured that the children had a real taste of farm and country magic and made friends with the cows.

Westminster schoolchildren, 1972. John Skerry, producer at Dorking WI Market, welcomes children to his farm, as part of the Town and Country project.

RESOLUTIONS FROM 1969–1975

More resolutions are brought by individuals or Federations than by the NFWI Executive. In Kesteven, in Lincolnshire, the village of Barrowby reacted strongly to the prospect of even larger and heavier vehicles thundering along country lanes. The Executive, too, urged the formulation of a comprehensive transport policy, something successive governments seem unable to devise. However, the creation of the action group Transport 2000 to lobby for the rationalization of transport needs gave the NFWI a body with which it still works closely; it is chaired in the 1990s by Suzanne May, former NFWI Hon. Treasurer.

The adoption of children in foster care was urged by Clearwell WI in Gloucesterhire, and Middlesex Executive recognized the financial difficulties of many mothers by urging that tax credits should be paid directly to mothers if family allowances ceased.

With a more permissive attitude to discussion of such matters, Anglesey Federation raised a subject that received overwhelming support: that advice on family planning should be freely available within the NHS. The West Sussex Federation urged WI members themselves to undertake to do all they could to prevent further damage from pollution in their own areas, and Leigh WI in Surrey called for intensified research into biodegradable packaging as part of the anti-pollution campaign.

'...undertake to do all they could to prevent further damage from pollution in their own areas...'

The inadequacy of rural transport and the threat to village post offices led Chignalls and Mashbury WIs, Essex, to launch a fight to save them which still continues at the present time. A further attempt to improve rural life was initiated by Stokenchurch WI, Buckinghamshire, which called for community facilities to be incorporated in new housing developments. But it was the NFWI Executive which asked the movement to seek financial aid for opposers of planning applications, as a means of permitting full public participation in planning procedures.

In the light of continued undermanning of the police force when an accelerating crime rate was causing public alarm, Whitchurch WI, Somerset, called for better pay and conditions for policemen. Closer to the heart of the WI, the NFWI Executive asked that crafts should be awarded equal status with the arts in the terms of government support. In consequence, responsibility for crafts was transferred to a newly formed Crafts Council, with greatly improved funding for the artist craft worker.

'...crafts should be awarded equal status with the arts...'

RESOLUTIONS FROM 1975–1977

The increase in crimes against women began to dominate the news in the late Seventies, but women suffering sexual assaults still experienced difficulty in bringing charges. The law was not only lenient; it caused further harm by making it permissible to question a victim's moral character.

In 1975 the NFWI suported a resolution brought by Farnham WI, Essex, to change the wording of the law relating to rape. Changes made by 1976 ensured a somewhat fairer balance. At the same meeting the situation of women suffering violence in the home was also considered. The WI supported accommodation for battered wives. By 1979, with the establishment of many help organizations, domestic violence against women had been redefined as criminal.

The NFWI restated their belief in the principle of equality of opportunity and legal status for women and pledged themselves to work to achieve it. They also agreed to support day centres for the mentally ill discharged from hospitals. Northamptonshire Executive drew attention to the problems of the homeless and the lack of rented accommodation, now even greater than it was at that time. The mandate still holds: Warwickshire Federation established its own housing association.

The NFWI Executive introduced a broad resolution asking the WI to pledge itself to intensify its policy of education in the production and preparation of food; it asked HM government to follow a stable, well-balanced agricultural policy for the country as a whole and, on a global scale, to support the UN in securing 'a more regular and even distribution of resources in the world at large'.

'...to support the UN in securing 'a more regular and even distribution of resources in the world at large...'

WI policy on this noble level has led to their working with ACWW, the UN, the European Union and the Overseas Development Administration, as well as offering continuing co-operation and support to farming organizations in our own country.

Continuing concern over the building of nuclear power generators, including the fast breeder reactor then under discussion, showed that the greatest anxiety was over the problem of disposing of nuclear waste. Not surprisingly, another resolution, calling for research into alternative sources of energy was overwhelmingly supported.

'...research into alternative sources of energy was overwhelmingly supported...'

RESOLUTIONS FROM 1977–1981

Although the supply of violent and pornographic reading material in circulation had been deplored in the Fifties, the increase in volume together with the general tendency of the popular press to focus on sex and crime caused Cambridgeshire Federation to urge all responsible persons to be aware of the dangers of such material as 'harmful to young minds'. At the same time an upswing in violent crime again resulted in a call, from Lowdham WI, Nottinghamshire, for the introduction of stronger deterrents, and a rise in underage drinking resulted in a call for more education in the dangers of alcohol.

The complexities of the tax system and social security laws brought a heartfelt cry for simplification from the NFWI – which cannot be said to have been much heeded!

Basic concern for the safety and quality of what we eat led Dunkerton WI, Avon, to draw attention to the dangers of inadequate labelling of frozen food, and Colehill WI in Dorset awakened a certain patriotic emotion when they called on their fellow members to 'do all in their power to maintain national varieties of fruit, vegetable and farm crops'.

'...do all in their power to maintain national varieties of fruit, vegetable and farm crops...'

Brixham WI, Devon, urged international monitoring of over-exploitation of marine life and the dangers of pollution, a subject since firmly established on the international agenda. In 1977 Threlkeld WI in Cumbria stressed the need for more day centres and aftercare for patients discharged from hospitals for the mentally ill. Although the discharge of patients into the community has accelerated in the last decade and WIs support the day care centres in their areas, this is still an active mandate.

RESOLUTIONS FROM 1981–1988

The pattern of resolutions coming to General Meetings reflects changes in social concern. Because of a rise in awareness of cases of child abuse, it was to be expected that it would gain from a women's organization. Two resolutions, in 1984 and 1986, both from Northumberland WIs, urged women to be alert to the problem, and the authorities to impose stiffer penalties for offences against children. And Sefton WI in Lancashire urged a similar response to cases of rape.

On the other hand. not all reactions to social problems called for punishment; some were positive. Crickhowell in Powis-Brecknock urged fellow members to support campaigns on AIDS and Wentworth Park, County Durham, brought the issue of solvent abuse to debate. In each case the call was for information, awareness and greater education. Hyde and Frogham WI, Hampshire, called for greater help and support for drug addicts and their families.

'...in each case the call was for information, awareness and greater education...'

Recognizing greater equality between husband and wife, Starcross WI in Devon asked that married women should be able to seek provision in their occupational pensions for their husbands should they predecease them. And Filkins and Broughton Poggs WI in Oxfordshire, noting a significant change in the national attitude towards thrift, urged more control of the 'aggressive and indiscriminate sale of credit' and 'more publicity as to the hazards of borrowing money'.

'...more control of the 'aggressive and indiscriminate sale of credit' and 'more publicity as to the hazards of borrowing money...'

Stranger subjects appeared on the agenda with the acceleration of scientific advance. What, asked Lincolnshire South Federation, of the legal status of artificially produced human embryos? A decade later Butts Brow WI, East Sussex, called for the rejection of a European Union directive authorizing the patenting of life forms, until the many implications had been debated. On the world stage, Woodsetts WI, South Yorkshire, called for a long-term programme of technical and financial assistance to increase the agricultural self-sufficiency of Third World countries.

The fragile nature of the planet was slowly being recognized by a wider public than the scientific community. Alert to the dangers of acid rain, Surlingham WI in Norfolk voiced the general concern in calling for reduced emissions of sulphur and nitrogen oxides from power stations, while Corfe WI in Somerset brought matters closer to home by asking members to discourage manufacturers from the use of chlorofluoro-carbons and by calling for their labelling, to slow down the depletion of the ozone layer.

Glenawr Glyn WI in Dyfed Caredigion, deploring the deforestation of the earth's surface, called for all to impress on government the need to halt excessive damage done to the ecological balance of our planet. Showing similar anxiety, Gillingham WI in Dorset urged stricter control on the importation, treatment and disposal of toxic wastes.

RESOLUTIONS FROM 1988–1994

In the general area of health, especially where it concerns women, support for hospices, for research into the causes and treatment of osteoporosis, and awareness of the dangers of paracetamol were all issues raised by WIs in the late Eighties. Many counties already assisted in various ways in research programmes concerned with health problems for women.

'...many counties already assisted in various ways in research programmes concerned with health problems for women...'

There are now fewer resolutions coming forward on new topics as WI policy based on existing mandates is broad and far-reaching and follow-up work is continuous, but concern for the future of our planet is perennial. Glemsford WI in Suffolk brought forward a motion urging HM Government to persuade other countries party to the Antarctic Treaty that Antarctica be declared a wilderness park, with military activity and the extraction of oil and minerals forbidden. This resolution was passed and then pursued relentlessly in conjunction with Greenpeace and the Worldwide Fund for Nature.

Initially, government response was less than wholehearted, and continuous pressure, together with visits to the Secretary of State for the Environment, produced less support than was needed. The thirty-year

Photograph of Eggleston Abbey by Mrs E A Sidaway, Stainton & Streatham WI displaying the WI's concern for the countryside.

Somerset Federation's superbly decorated version of the WI anthem, William Blake's "Jerusalem".

Antarctic treaty was about to expire and the government favoured a minerals convention legalizing mineral exploration and extraction. NFWI, Greenpeace and WWF protested and sought a ministerial meeting which helped to persuade the government to change its mind and to support a proposed moratorium. The three organizations were additionally successful in helping government to enlist the support of the United States. Eventually an Environment Protocol affording protection for 50 years was signed in Madrid in October 1991. Antarctica has still not been granted World Park status, but 50 years is a good start and gives time to ensure that the ban on exploitation becomes permanent.

Water policy, a variation on a constant WI theme, was once again raised by Blewbury WI in Oxfordshire, calling for the protection and preservation of the country's rivers, streams and ponds and the promotion of long-term planning and co-operation between regions. The Welsh Federations, in the meantime, had initiated a nationwide water project, each WI undertaking the maintenance or restoration of a local water feature. Many streams, springs, wells and ponds were the beneficiaries.

Demonstrating the natural aversion of countrywomen to the misuse of land, South Lincolnshire Federation called for more research into the

'...a nationwide water project, each WI undertaking the maintenance or restoration of a local water feature...'

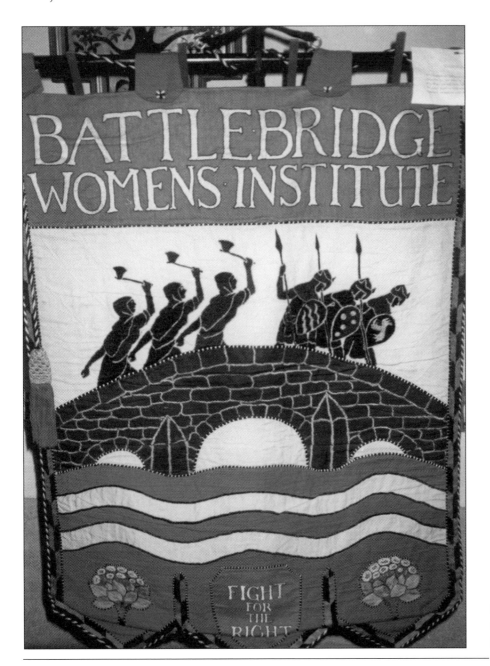

Battlebridge WI's banner reflects the determination of the WI as a whole to "fight for the right".

use of food crops in surplus, and of non-food crops for industrial use, 'to obviate the need for set-aside'.

The increase in crime once again caused concern. Old Heathfield in Sussex won support for compulsory DNA testing where it might assist in the solving of violent crimes.. Clare WI in Suffolk wanted a review of the Homicide Act so that the definition of provocation should include prolonged domestic violence; NFWI members lobbied Parliament to good effect in the company of other women's groups.

'...the movement is seen as a rich source of information...'

In 1990 the NFWI produced a Countryside Policy document, the product of a survey on rural life made by Federations throughout the country. The survey covered the rural economy, the future of agriculture, rural housing, health, transport and education. The movement is seen as a rich source of information and much of the work was in response to requests from government departments and outside bodies.

By 1994 rural life had undergone great changes. Village shops, medical services, schools and transport services are under threat or lost already. Neighbours no longer meet on the local bus, at the doctor's surgery or while buying stamps or household provisions. Houses change hands at prices beyond the reach of young local people and weekend cottages or the influx of urban outsiders hastens the death of traditional village life. The WI is often the last thing left in the village to draw its inhabitants together and maintain any sense of community.

'...the WI is often the last thing left in the village to draw its inhabitants together and maintain any sense of community...'

Recently there have been a number of time-consuming resolutions concerned with turning the WI into a charitable company but by 1994 it was possible to return to public affairs, and three of the topics dealt with had legal implications.

Having expressed their support for organ donation for transplants, WIs wished to simplify the process of using human organs for saving the lives of others. Under the existing system it is still necessary to obtain permission from next of kin. The movement felt that a simpler and more direct system should be devised.

Proposed changes in the legal aid system were received with dismay. It was felt that the new level of income at which people would be entitled to aid would place legal representation beyond the reach of all but the very poor or the very rich, undermining the concept of justice for all.

'...the concept of justice for all...'

The third 1994 mandate pressed for a less confusing definition of material of an explicit and violent content than can be found in existing legislation. It was felt that the present criteria are such that the legal test is unworkable.

4: DUMPSY DEARY VERSUS THE SUPERSTORE
The story of WI Markets

WE are in a sports hall. At one end is a boxing ring. At the other are tables laden with a cornucopian display of farm and kitchen produce. Buckets of fresh flowers perfume the air. Jars of preserves gleam softly and temptingly. Busy people, mostly women but some men, check deliveries, arrange appetizing displays of cakes and pies, set out the cash point, gather their order forms and ready themselves for an eagerly awaited and most good-humoured of frays.

It is 10.30 a.m. Near the boxing ring a rope holds back a friendly, chattering throng. A steward looks at her colleagues. 'Ready?' she asks then moves towards the crowd and unfastens the rope. There is a surge forward. It's just like the beginning of a marathon. The hall is in Wells, Somerset, and it isn't a marathon but a normal start to trading in the on-going success story of a WI market day.

'...it isn't a marathon but a normal start to trading in the on-going success story of a WI market day...'

The first WI retail market started in Lewes, East Sussex, in 1919, to help ex-servicemen and the unemployed make the most of their allotments. It created a valuable opportunity for turning smallholdings and the domestic skills of cooking and preserving into a source of profit and a means of supplementing the family budget of suppliers. Other markets soon followed.

In 1932, after an appeal from the Ministry of Agriculture to increase home production of foodstuffs, such markets became an official WI activity. This meant that standards could be set, order established and procedures harmonized wherever markets were set up. From the beginning it was not only WI members who were involved, and in any case, the WI, as a charity, is not allowed to trade. Marketing co-operatives, which could be registered under the Industrial Provident and Friendly Societies Act, were the solution to the problem.

'...standards could be set, order established and procedures harmonized wherever markets were set up...'

Anyone wishing to trade can become a market shareholder by purchasing a share for a small sum. Individuals may become shareholders; so may groups such as WIs themselves, Allotment Societies or Village Produce Associations.

The producers make money from their hard work, and a percentage of their takings goes to meet the overhead expenses of the market. The Markets Department of the NFWI was created with a grant from the UK Carnegie Trust and there is a National Market Adviser to oversee all market activities.

All Federations have Voluntary County Markets Organizers (VCMOs) who are responsible for the markets in their Federation. The Federations pay their expenses; the markets donate the costs of training.

But there's a lot more to it than that. Very often the only part of the WI instantly recognizable to the general public is the nearest market, so the standards of professionalism and the quality of the produce reflect on the reputation of the WI as a whole.

'...even those who know nothing about the WI know about WI markets...'

Even those who know nothing about the WI know about WI markets. The sight of a cheerfully patient queue with empty baskets waiting outside a village hall or in a market-place is an indication that this is WI market day. Since the customers are nearly all regulars, it is not surprising that they, and the market helpers too, tend to become old friends.

'One of our regular customers,' relates Betty Walker of Wells, 'was an old man who was always losing his money through a hole in his coat pocket, so after several weeks of this we took it off him and repaired it while he shopped.'

Markets can be held in covered market halls, as for example in Chichester, where they have their own lock-up premises. They may operate from church halls near the main shopping street of the town, as in Bath or Dorking, or they may have their own shop, like Taunton.

'...it is market policy never to undercut shop prices...'

To avoid alienating local shopkeepers it is market policy never to undercut shop prices, and established traders quickly find that a new

WI Market parcels waiting delivery at Bovingdon and District WI Market, Hertfordshire, Christmas, 1994.

market is not a rival but an additional amenity, attracting new custom to the area, to their general benefit.

Customers track down WI markets wherever they trade and introduce their friends: their reputation is formidable. They sell the produce of garden, allotment, farm or smallholding, and, of course, of countless kitchens. They set unsurpassed standards for homebaked bread, preserves, cakes, pastries and savoury dishes, game, poultry, cream, cheeses, fruit, plants and flowers.

In addition there is often a craft stall, with handmade woollens, lace, embroidery and similar hand-crafted goods. All are of a very high standard since, as with everything sold under the WI aegis, they would otherwise be rejected by the controller.

It is the controller who reigns supreme in each individual market. Every market society has its own elected committee and, for the actual running of the weekly operation, a controller, stall helpers, and, equally important, a treasurer. Helpers are very often producers themselves, although they do not need to be. There's a superficial 'playing at shops' aspect to running a market which has a natural appeal. For one thing,

Above left: Crafts from WI Markets at the East of England Show, July 1994.
Above right: Freshly baked breads are a Market's best seller.

it's only once a week, and it's an event: the same people gather and greet each other. It quickly becomes a tradition and a routine, though the setting up and opening of each market is a hectic and onerous business.

'...alive with the noise of children from the room next-door where the playgroup meets...'

A typical small market is Freshford in Avon. Open for business twice a month, in a bright village hall, it's alive with the noise of children from the room next-door where the playgroup meets. The mums take advantage of the coffee served by the market and are regular customers at the stalls; many of them are vegetarian and dishes are home-cooked specially for them by Diana Agorriz.

A mother of grown sons and a daughter, Diana found it strange to adjust to cooking for just two when the family moved on to university. Each week a regular supply of dishes emerges from her kitchen: moussakas, lentil loaves, ratatouille, cheese flans and pies. 'But nothing with rice. That's the biggest health hazard. Unless it's freshly cooked the day it's eaten, there's a danger of salmonella and we can't risk that.'

'...what happens to the yolks?...'

Pauline Bates makes meringues. How many? 'Oh, I do them all the week; about three trays a day, that's 50. Sealed in packs of six, they keep well.' What happens to the yolks? An obvious question from another cook. 'Paté sucrée, savoury flans, fruit flans, about twelve to eighteen flans a week.'

Libby Kerr prefers savouries; she makes many varieties of savoury bread; sunflower seed, sun-dried tomato, rosemary and walnut, olive and herbs. Any problem persuading customers to try things they may not have seen before? 'Ah, we had a taster day a few weeks ago. Everyone made extra which we gave away as samples and saw what went well, what people liked.'

'...they prefer home-cooked food, and knowing it's wholesome...'

Not all the helpers are WI members; all are shareholders and members of the Market Society. They are very much aware of their service to the community. Many customers are without readily available transport to the nearest supermarket. 'Anyway, they prefer home-cooked food, and knowing it's wholesome.' And as for elderly, often single-person households, 'We do lots of one-person dishes, quiches and pies, then they just have to heat them up and there's no waste.'

Assistant controller, Jane Vaisey, arrives at 8.30 a.m. to get the tables out and to check in. 'There's the invoices to check off, that takes two of us. At the end they have to be checked again with anything not sold crossed off, then they go to the treasurer ready to be paid for at the end of the month.' How much does the average producer make? 'Money or goods? On the whole, around £100 a month but, of course, there's the cost of ingredients to subtract from that.'

Chesterfield WI Market, Derbyshire, sets out its plants.

For producers the income is a valuable supplement to their income. Service to the community is an important factor which ranks high in any list of WI priorities. Customers come in for advice on gardening matters as well as a chat. The Royal Botanical Gardens at Kew, no less, have asked WI markets to look out for certain plants which seem to have become rare or even disappeared. There is always the possibility that they will turn up on the stall of a grower who may not be a botanist but has little to learn about horticulture.

'... rare plants for Kew Gardens...'

Women – men too – living on their own look for one-person dishes. Undomesticated but discriminating students come in to stock up for the week. One anxious and generous mother had a parcel delivered to her student son in every one of the six weeks during which he was sitting his final exams. It was to meet such needs that the WI Markets parcel scheme was introduced.

Initially planned to make up produce parcels to order for local people or for customers who wanted to send an unusual present to friends, later, in the form of 'Happiness Hampers', it was extended to people with special needs. In a further development of this service, parcels can now be ordered in one area for delivery in another: any market can arrange the transfer.

'...'Happiness Hampers' can now be ordered in one area for delivery in another...'

Talking of friends, those markets where nearby WIs supplement their own funds by making coffee in rotation have established their own regular clientele. They become meeting places for young mums whose babies grow up under the benevolent eyes of adopted aunties whose interest may compensate for the lack of nearby relatives.

In some quarters there used to be a feeling that making money for one-self out of the WI was really 'not quite nice'. Though markets in Yorkshire, for example, flourished during the Second World War, they all closed down afterwards. Fortunately they are now flourishing again; women today have no inhibitions about working to supplement the family budget. It's not only 'nice' to earn money, it's enormously satisfying for the ego as well as good for the purse.

'...women today have no inhibitions about working to supplement the family budget...'

From the very beginning it was a matter of pride to keep within the law and on good terms with those who regulate trading. The market advisers keep up to date with every change and nuance but now and then there are small clashes of views. Well, sometimes not so small. In one celebrated case the full powers of law and parliament were brought into action!

In 1980 a change in the law required market traders to register their premises if they wished to sell their produce to the public. When a market was set up in Stockton, on Teesside, no such law existed, but they dutifully contacted the local Environmental Health department to ensure that no regulations would be infringed.

'..."you're breaking the law"...'

'Ah-ha!' was the response. 'All preserved foods must be made on registered premises only. If you sell homemade preserves, you're breaking the law.' Consternation! Hundreds of markets nationwide had been selling preserves for sixty years. This was the first time it had ever been suggested that the WI were criminals.

Legal advice was taken at National level on what constituted preserved food. The problem was publicized and the publicity became red-hot. Letters flooded in to Ruth Studholme, a farmer's wife from Thorpe Thewles, near Stockton, who was at the heart of the storm, and she decided to fight the ban.

'...the first time it had ever been suggested that the WI were criminals...the matter was raised in the House of Commons in Westminster...'

The case was brought to the attention of European Member of Parliament, Sir Peter Vanneck. He asked questions of the European Commission and in no time at all the matter was raised in the House of Commons in Westminster.

The consequence was Early Day Motion 702 on 12 June, 1980, which said: This House congratulates the Women's Institutes on their continued loyal service to the nation, sends its greetings and sincerely hopes that they will continue to make their excellent jams and pickles in spite of the intervention of bureaucracy.

The following day, Nicholas Winterton MP asked Patrick Jenkins, Secretary of State for Agriculture, Fisheries and Food, whether he was satisfied with the registration provisions of the Foods and Drugs Act 1955 so far as they concerned the preparation of homemade jams for sale. The Secretary of State, praising the long and honoured tradition of WI members in the sale of jam and other home-made products, said he did not believe that any interpretation of the Act was intended to interfere with it.

Mrs Ruth Studholme, Mrs Agnes Salter, and a delegation were invited to take their products to the House of Commons so that MPs could taste a selection of the famous jams. They were naturally pronounced delicious, and after the tasting session Mr Charles Irving MP, Chairman of the House of Commons catering sub-committee, ordered two tons of jam for parliamentary consumption.

'...two tons of jam for parliamentary consumption...'

The Secretary of State was handed a letter asking for his help in amending the law and Gerry Neale MP promised to bring in a Private Member's Bill in the then session of parliament; the amendment would become law if a ten-minute speech were made and no one disagreed with its content. No one did.

On 15 May the Bill went to the House of Lords where it received its second reading unopposed. In July 1981 the Royal assent was given, exempting WI market cooks from having to register their kitchens with the local authority.

Below left: Crafts from WI Markets, County Show, May 1990.
Below right: WI Market display at Cranleigh and Woking, Surrey, March 1990.

On 17 July 1981, a year and one month after the beginning of the controversy but only fifteen weeks after the introduction of the Bill,

Celebration cake stall, Ledbury WI
Market (Hereford)

'...WI markets have a responsible attitude toward public health and produce food of the very highest standard...'

Stockton market sold its first lawful jam, having demonstrated in no uncertain fashion that WI markets have a responsible attitude toward public health and produce food of the very highest standard. The enormous amount of publicity generated showed how formidable the movement can be in marshalling support for a rightful cause.

Now that we are a member state of the European Union there are even more regulations to observe, but there are also new opportunities to be seized. When Jan Holmes, secretary of Hampshire WI Markets, heard about the 'Best of British' Market on the waterfront in Cherbourg, she couldn't wait to test the water. 'We wanted to publicize the markets,' she said, 'and see how viable it would be for WI market goods.'

Since an exploratory trip would be expensive, the produce she took was mainly her own and that of a fellow-producer from Alton market. Items included toys and over 700 jars of preserves. The typically bitter-sweet taste of English marmalades proved so popular that only half a dozen jars remained unsold, and three local restaurants have placed orders for marmalade to go with their English breakfasts. As Jan said, 'It's a wonderful way to look for new markets and combine a holiday.'

'...a wonderful way to look for new markets and combine a holiday...'

One thing is certain: whenever the WI is on parade, as for instance at a county agricultural event or the Royal Show, a WI market is an enormous crowd puller. One of the special strengths of the markets lies in their individual and regional differences, and producers have their own jealously guarded secrets. 'They will give you a smile, they will give you advice, but they won't part with their recipes.' And why on earth should they, indeed?

At the Ideal Home exhibition in 1965, the WI's Golden Jubilee year, the eager crowds so besieged the stall that the helpers were almost overwhelmed, although fresh supplies were brought in daily from markets all over the country to meet the demand. The top seller was Dumpsy

Princess Alice visits WI Markets at East of England Show, July 1994.

Deary jam – a Worcestershire recipe based on apples, pears and plums with lemon zest and ginger – of which customers seemingly could not get enough. There's no telling, thirty years later, how it would go down in Cherbourg.

One carload of eggs from Dorking market, aiming to reach Olympia in good time to unload, broke down on Hammersmith Bridge and arrived too late to reach the inside car park. The team had to park in the street and walk right through the exhibition hall with tray after tray of eggs, all of which they delivered safely before donning their overalls and beginning to serve the crowds.

'...market producers take changes and difficulties in their stride...'

It's a measure of the strengths and adaptability of the market producers that they take changes and difficulties in their stride. Faint hearts may have thought that all the changing rules and regulations would make it impossible for them to continue, or would rob them of that special humanity which makes them unique, but they flourish. They have marched on from that first market in Lewes, not always serenely, not always without difficulty, but nevertheless from strength to strength.

Producers and helpers alike are great survivors and great adapters. Most that is typical of country living has gone from the towns. It is even diminishing in the villages, but WI markets have taken over the Windmill Theatre's famous wartime slogan: We never close. In these days of superstores and out-of-town shopping malls, when so many high street shops have gone to the wall, it is the very 'hands-on' quality of WI markets that makes them a joy, a blessing, and a national institution.

A Taste of WI Markets, published by WI Books to celebrate 75 years of homemade cooking; all the recipes are well-tried favourites of Market members.

5: DENMAN, THE CREATIVE DYNAMO

DENMAN College in the village of Marcham, Oxfordshire, is the WI movement's creative and cultural dynamo; an educational centre, a beautiful country house and a social focus. But the notion of the WI having a house of their own, of running a college, of having a centre for holding conferences under their own control, was not a sudden inspiration.

The idea of a college, first considered by National Federation educational organizers during the Second World War, was discussed privately and tentatively before any further action was taken. In 1943 a residential conference was held at Radbrook College, Shrewsbury to discuss the revolutionary Beveridge Report, already a major topic in every part of the land. A guest speaker, Sir Richard Livingstone, distinguished educationalist and president of Corpus Christi college, Oxford, asked Federation representatives a pre-planned question.

After criticizing the government for setting out ideas for education which were to lead to the Education Act of 1944, while making no plans for adult education, he said, 'Why should not the Women's Institutes fill the gap? Why don't you start a people's college yourselves?' The purpose was to judge reactions among the audience of about 100. No one blenched. There was a murmur of interested surmise. Discussion followed and plans were made to put the thought to the National Executive and the members.

Denman College, Oxfordshire. Dreamed of in wartime and realized in peace.

'...why don't you start a people's college yourselves?...'

Students relax between classes in the library at Denman, before conversion to include the bar.

At the Annual General Meeting in 1945 Lady Brunner of the Oxfordshire Federation proposed that 'this meeting welcomes the suggestion of a Women's Institute college ... and instructs the Executive to make the necessary arrangements'.

Some were dubious and many highly nervous at what was being undertaken, but the visionaries managed to carry the day. A year later NFWI Executive launched an appeal to raise the money to translate dream into reality.

The Carnegie Trust had already promised generous support; the Countess of Albemarle, Lady Denman's successor as NFWI Chairman, was also a life trustee. One of the points used to reassure members of the practicability of embarking on the great undertaking was that the government would be obliged to include adult education in its plans.

Below right: Two new cottages, Willow and Beech, opened 1993. Below left: The Dining Room at Denman.

In the event, no government grants were forthcoming for the founding of the college but the Department of Education did promise support

Graham Jones, Principal, speaking at the opening of Beech and Willow by Lady Brunner (left) and Lady Anglesey (right), 1993.

once the college was established and the programme was under way. The Carnegie Trust was firm in its commitment to provide £20,000. The target for the first fund was £60,000, a great sum for those days. This, it was hoped, would pay for a suitable house, for rebuilding and furnishing, and leave something over to subsidize course fees.

Already Lady Brunner, now Chairman of the College Committee, and her team were looking everywhere for a possible building. After considering a great variety of properties a possible and available one came on the market.

Marcham Park, in a quiet and charming village not far from Oxford, was a gracious house with sixteen bedrooms and adequate bathrooms, a good hall and reception rooms. It had been occupied by the RAF during the war and there were still Nissen huts in the grounds but its potential was obvious. It was bought, inclusive of gardens, 100 acres of land and two cottages, for £16,000.

Since Lady Denman's retirement as Chairman of the National Federation was anounced at the same Annual General Meeting that had passed the resolution to look for a college, it was decided to commemorate her chairmanship appropriately. Marcham Park immediately became Denman College-to-be.

It was not only going to 'make provision to advance education' still further but was also to become a focus of interest and activity for members as the nation itself wrestled with severe rationing, postwar exhaustion and, paradoxically, euphoria as an idealistic new government and people embarked upon the creation of the welfare state.

'...make provision to advance education... to become a focus of interest and activity...'

There was to be a brave new world, and countrywomen were determined to play their part in creating it.

With courage and optimism they set about the task of paying for and furnishing their house. The Federations accepted the challenge with enthusiastic delight; competition was keen to be allotted a bedroom to furnish to their own plan and colour scheme. Even to refurbish their own homes was difficult enough in those hard times; there were shortages of almost everything except ideas, but those were plentiful and could be lavished on their new communal acquisition.

Each bedroom at Denman is furnished by a different County Federation.

Each Federation equipped its allocated room with curtains, bedspreads, handiwork, tapestry, pictures, rugs, work-boxes, lamps, cushions; anything that would create an ambience of care and comfort. The crafts were usually characteristic of the appropriate county, to leave future occupants in no doubt as to which Federation's room they were staying

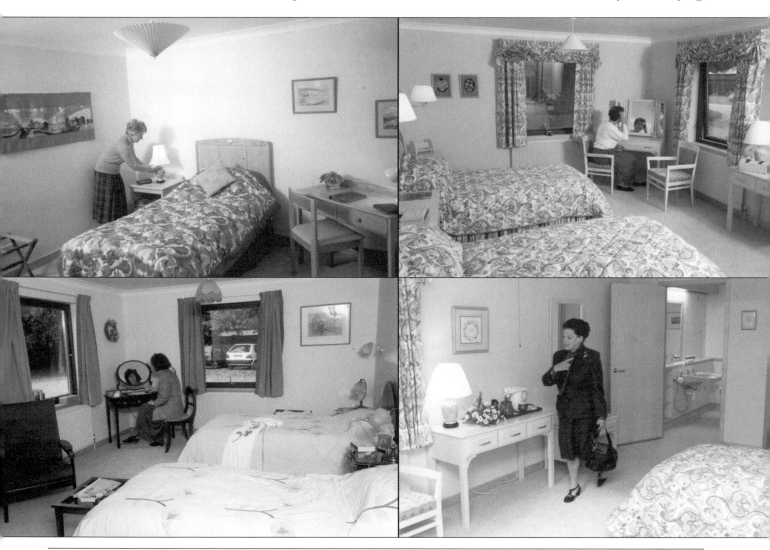

Agnes Salter, NFWI Chairman, on the main staircase of Denman College, with students and tutor.

in. Such artistry made the mansion a unique treasurehouse, and so it remains to this day.

As everything was still rationed, some furnishings owed much to ingenuity. The dining-room curtains were tablecloths from Lady Denman's Australian Government House days, handblocked in patterns of prancing unicorns. The hall floors were livened with rugs of Norfolk reed made by Norfolk members. The drawing-room had eighteenth-century furniture, another gift from Lady Denman. Throughout the house selections of paintings loaned by artist friends such as Edward Bawden and John Aldridge brightened the walls. By courtesy of the Victoria and Albert Museum a display of historic embroidery was on show in the library when the college opened for its first students.

'...some furnishings owed much to ingenuity...'

That was not until 1948, after two years of battling to win licences for the materials and the permits needed to get necessary work done. At first the teaching rooms were out in the grounds in the RAF's abandoned Nissen huts. Rechristened Homeacres, they served their purpose for nearly twenty years. There was no suitable demonstration kitchen but students went 'down the road' to Abingdon College of Further Education.

As an establishment the college is wholly owned by the National Federation of Women's Institutes. It was set up as a trust, with Lady Albemarle and Lady Brunner as named trustees to carry the financial responsibility. The management was delegated to a House Committee appointed by the NF Executive, the first chairman being Lady Brunner until she herself became National Chairman.

The management committee in its turn appointed staff to take over the day-to-day running of what was partly a college, a place of learning, and partly an on-going and purposeful country house party whose guests changed every four days, involving adroit handling on the housekeeping front.

'...partly a college, a place of learning, and partly an on-going and purposeful country house party...'

It was decided, following the example of many of the colleges of neighbouring Oxford, that Denman's 'head' should be called the Warden. The first appointee was the happily-named Elizabeth Christmas. Betty Christmas, previously NFWI general organizer for eight years, was a friendly, bubbly character who was to be central to the creation of the warm, welcoming atmosphere which is still so much a part of 'the Denman experience'. She, together with a bursar and the domestic staff, indoor and outdoor, ran a tight ship.

Below right: Dancing on the lawn at the 1992 Festival.
Below left: The Drawing Room.

The academic programme was initially drawn up by the NFWI education sub-committee. They didn't lack for advice from distinguished educationalists, but establishing the balance among all the special interests of

the WI members they were setting out to attract was something they felt only other WI members would be able to do.

Later, when additional accommodation had been created in the former stables, and three courses could be run at a time with over fifty students living in, a resident tutor joined the staff. It is easy to imagine that the demands of receiving new guests and overseeing day-to-day management does not exactly leave much room for acting the gracious hostess. This had been foreseen, however, and the role of course chairman, in rotation, was filled by members and past members of the National Executive and sub-committees, and county committees.

The present rôle of College Chairman is to welcome students, deal with personal problems and generally assist in creating a happy and homely atmosphere.

The first courses at Denman ranged from the purely practical to the artistic and intellectual. Students worked hard; they were not going to waste time when they only had four or five hard-won days away from home and family. And having three or four different courses running simultaneously guaranteed an interesting exchange of ideas at breaks and mealtimes.

Above: Part of a flower display in the Library, when arrangers adorned the whole house.

Below: Relaxing over a drink before dinner at Denman – a wonderful opportunity to chat with fellow WI members.

Students, then as now, were a mixture much as in individual WIs. Speakers, then as now, ranged over a wide spectrum of skills and subjects: on a single course there were an Oxford don, a bookseller, a novelist, sessions on musical appreciation, poetry readings, a recorder-playing session, and a visit to the Bodleian Library. Such variety leads to a well-spiced life.

'...such variety leads to a well-spiced life...'

The initial trickle of courses and students swelled to a steady stream. As one year's programmes got under way the next was already in course of preparation. Students went back to their WIs full of enthusiasm and encouraged their friends to follow their example. And for every one actually taking a course there were many who were curious to see what it was like: what had all their fund-raising efforts produced and had the money been well spent?

The college closed for two weeks in July for annual cleaning and maintenance work, but the house and grounds remained open for parties of members from all over the country to pay their visits, have tea in their college and perhaps, in due course, take the decision to go there as students themselves.

It was essential to keep up the interest. The available resources ebbed and flowed, with perhaps too much ebb and not sufficient flow. Nevertheless, visitors were usually pleased with the success of their investment, as was the Chairman of the Carnegie Trust, when, in 1949, he came to open the newly converted stable block, 'The Croft'. 'I have never,' he enthused, 'seen a more living and striking example of community life in practice than in this beautiful college.'

'...I have never seen a more living and striking example of community life in practice than in this beautiful college...'

Gifts, frequently memorials for past members, were made to the college, including its grounds, where an avenue of limes was planted to commemorate the redoubtable Mrs Watt whose enthusiasm had breathed life into the very first WIs. But the endowment fund, which had been expected to underpin expenses for many years, did not grow as fast as did the ambition to expand. The college income, apart from student fees, was £1,000 a year from the Ministry of Education and £1,500 from the endowment fund. There was no capital fund for maintenance or replacement.

In 1956 Lady Denman died. As WIs wished to show their respect, affection and gratitude for her years of guidance, a fund came into being and grew rapidly. As one tribute to her memory it was decided to rebuild the dining room. The remainder of the fund was invested to yield an income for bursaries and for the general upkeep of the college. It was a year of sadness as well as change, for Elizabeth Christmas also died and it was necessary to appoint a new Warden.

The Queen opens the Home Economics Centre at Denman, 1979. NFWI Chairman, Patricia Batty-Shaw, H.M., Treasurer Kate Foss, General Secretary Anne Ballard, and Principal Hilda Jones.

The programme was still planned by the education sub-committee, with suggestions from the Federations. 'A' courses were run for any student who wished to take them. 'B' courses were introduced for members who would take them on behalf of their Federation, on the understanding that they would then go back and pass their knowledge on.

A later example of a 'B' course was one put on by the NFWI to mark European Architectural Heritage Year. The chairman and deviser of that course was Freda Gwylliam, one of many gifted people who have given their service to the WI having already had distinguished careers; she was co-opted on to the NFWI Executive on her retirement as Chief Education Officer for the Ministry of Overseas Development.

Freda was an inspiring teacher, not least to those who had the pleasure of working with her. 'Remember,' she would say, 'always create an

'...remember, always create an on-going situation...'

ongoing situation.' Everything must lead somewhere. Students at Denman might only go for a few days, but should leave inspired to follow another path and spurred on to further study.

'...the variety of course subjects continued to combine the practical with the academic...'

The variety of course subjects continued to combine the practical with the academic. Crafts predominated but art, music and drama gradually increased. 1957 saw a course on 'Writing a Village History' and, for the first time, a course on science.

The latter certainly created an ongoing situation, as many of the participants, stimulated by what they had learned, went back to organize similar courses in their own counties. In the Nineties science courses are surging ahead, but in the Sixties and Seventies, Pat Jacobs, a member of the Denman committee and a future National Chairman, had to argue strongly for further such courses before it became generally accepted that scientific understanding is an essential part of the mental equipment of an educated person. In consequence the NFWI was made an honorary corporate member of the British Association for the Advancement of Science, and some members of Executive are able to attend its annual conference.

But by 1960 inflation was eroding the endowment fund and the NFWI was obliged to make up the deficiency in the college budget. Lady Anglesey, as College Chairman, launched another Denman Appeal, this time with a minimum target of £25,000.

By the end of 1961 the figure achieved had risen to £40,000. A year later an anonymous donation of £10,000 enabled a Benefaction Fund to be created to support the educational work of the college.

During the years following the death of Betty Christmas a series of appointments was made to the post of Warden. Between 1958 and 1967 there was a rather high turnover, although each warden in turn introduced some new element into the life of the college. Cecily McCall, between 1958 and 1962, started Mothers and Babies courses which were a great success for the mothers and an equally great headache for the college staff. In due course they were replaced by Mothers and Daughters courses which were easier to run and are still very popular.

'...mothers and babies courses which were a great success for the mothers and an equally great headache for the college staff...'

In 1961 Hilda Jones joined the staff as the first Director of Studies, rather than tutor, and Marjorie Moller, the next Warden, introduced Federation courses, when a Federation could take over the entire college for the week. This overcame two problems, that of the nervous student who 'would love to come but would rather be with someone I know', and the cost of travel. Sufficient students from the same area made it possible to book coaches, which provided much the cheapest form of transport.

The courses already in the syllabus for that week offered a choice of at least three quite varied subjects. Ann Dolphin, 1964-67, increased the number of courses for creative writers and introduced co-ordinated courses, with related subjects running concurrently, so that there could be one or two joint sessions.

This creative overlapping was the idea of Hilda Jones, who felt that subjects should not always be 'kept in parcels'. Three courses harnessed in this fashion were 'The Modern Novel', 'Modern Painting' and 'Modern Sculpture'. In similar fashion pottery was allied with painting, and the contemporary novel with contemporary drama. Language courses of the 'brush up' variety were included at weekends.

'...creative overlapping ... subjects should not always be kept in parcels...'

The Denman College management committee, formed from the House and Education committees, had a great deal to do, running the college and devising the programmes. Once the courses had been decided it was up to the Director of Studies to find the lecturers and tutors.

In 1965, with the movement celebrating its Golden Jubilee, plans were at last made to replace all the old teaching rooms with a completely

Dry Stone Walling Course.

new block and additional accommodation for students. As so often has been the case with the movement, the money for the work would come 'later'. And so it did; yet another donation from an anonymous donor, this time for £30,000.

In 1967 Helen Anderson succeeded Ann Dolphin, arriving in time to oversee the building of the new teaching block. A series of hexagonal rooms with interesting lantern roofs to provide natural lighting were opened in 1969 by the Queen Mother. The buildings, following a familiar pattern, exceeded the budget, but Sir Felix and Lady Brunner made up the balance 'in order that standards shouldn't fall'.

'...in order that standards shouldn't fall...'

These revolutionary linking hexagons, not unlike a section of honey-comb and very attractive in appearance, blended beautifully with the grounds but proved quite difficult to adjust to at first, both for teaching in the one block and for sleeping in the other. Once the student accomodation was marked out, the rooms looked so small that the new Warden, Helen Anderson, lay on the bare earth in one of the hexagons to make quite sure that they really were going to accommodate a bed and an occupant.

Now so familiar to students and visitors, they initially experienced terrible teething troubles. With leaking roofs and a faulty heating system there were problems of cold on chilly days, and even greater problems with high temperatures when the sun shone. There was a day with the temperature in the nineties when Hilda Jones walked into a pottery class only to find students looking not only cool but positively smug: they all had their feet in bowls of cold water. WI members are nothing if not adaptable.

'...WI members are nothing if not adaptable...'

The week of the royal opening brought many visitors, members from all over the country arriving by the coachload to inspect their property and, though they may not have looked at it quite like that, to see if their money had been well spent. One day was also 'show-off' day, when visitors from all the local education authorities were invited, along with other friends in the educational world. So many of them, over the years, had given freely of their help, advice and influence to an establishment held in high esteem.

As courses have from the first mingled adventurous topics with the more orthodox, the field of lecturers willing to participate has been wide. The proximity of Oxford and Reading universities has been advantageous, but others have come from London, Leeds, Birmingham, Keele, St Andrews and Sussex. Encountering a student body which is adult, responsive and of enquiring mind, they find the teaching itself stimulating, and many come again and again.

Not long after the teaching block and Brunner House, the residential block, had been completed, plans went ahead for the new Home Econmics Centre which would be attached to the teaching block. Denman itself was 'an on-going situation' in the true Freda Gwyilliam style.

In the Seventies, in addition to the science courses, there were a number which examined the problems of the contemporary world. These included courses on the 'Order of St John of Jerusalem', the 'United Nations', the 'West Indies', followed by 'Democracy: its strengths and weaknesses', 'Economics and Ordinary People', and 'The Last 50 Years of Modern History'. In 1972 there were 'Our Common Market Neighbours' and 'The Races of Man'.

The traditional last night ceilidh sometimes gave way to general discussion; after a 'Modern Arts' week at which Lady Anglesey was course chairman she, artist Lawrence Bradbury and an expert from the Victoria and Albert Museum, all of whom had been lecturing, had a tremendous argument about modern art. 'It was a most animated and marvellous final session, very little from the students but a great deal from the panel!' recalls Helen Anderson.

Helen retired in 1977 after ten stimulating years in partnership with Hilda Jones. The Executive decided to ask Hilda to combine the functions of Warden and Director of Studies in the new post of first College Principal.

Once again new funds were acquired, the sale of the market garden providing money to commence the construction of the new kitchen building. 1978 was named Denman Birthday Year and it was put about

Above: NSPCC collage at Denman with another imaginative display.

Lady Albemarle lays the foundation stone to the Home Economics Centre at Denman.

The Queen opens the Home
Economics Centre at Denman.

that if anyone should contemplate a birthday present, something
towards this new building would not come amiss. The WIs responded
handsomely with presents totalling £28,000 and extra publicity for the
birthday and its underlying purpose came in a singularly apt way. Hilda
Jones, speaking at the Albert Hall AGM, was able to announce an
event that had been anticipated for days: the first brood of cygnets had
hatched on the college lake. They were promptly christened Andrew,
George and Megan: A, G and M.

*'...Her Majesty let it be known
that she would like the visit to be
informal...'*

The Queen agreed to open the new Home Economics Centre in 1979.
Her Majesty let it be known that she 'would like the visit to be informal', only for the organizers to discover that there was little difference
between planning and security for a formal and an informal occasion.
The only informality lay in the fact that the college and its courses
would run as near normally as possible. However, the informality did
extend to the Queen having the chance to look in on a few lessons,
even to having a friendly argument with the gardening tutor on the
best time of year to prune roses.

All this was progress indeed, but no matter how much money came in,
unexpectedly or through the devoted efforts of members all over the
country, there was – and still is – an insistent need for more.

Thus no sooner was one landmark in achievement reached without
disaster than another loomed. 1980 saw a record number of students.

Hilda was performing the dual rôle of running the college and overseeing the academic programme: she was also approaching retirement.

The Executive, also reorganizing, had decided to do away with the Denman College committee. The educational side was handled by the NFWI education co-ordinating group. A liaison officer, who was an NFWI committee member, acted as go-between with college staff, group and Executive. As the college was such a central part of WI life, the National chairman and treasurer regularly visited and consulted, but there was no direct governing body for the college itself.

The tenancy of the farmland and woodland bordering the college was discontinued, but maintenance of the boundary walls themselves became a considerable burden. Something had to be done; no one knew what; then another WI miracle took place.

Needlework (above) and Woodwork (below) courses at Denman.

During a 1980 conference at which the National chairman, treasurer and general secretary were present at the college there was a telephone call to Hilda Jones from Mrs Duffield, a neighbour and member of the family who had formerly owned Marcham Park. She had something of importance to discuss. The chairman and treasurer were duly summoned, having been told that the subject would concern them.

Mrs Duffield, in the words of Hilda Jones, 'said that her son was very anxious to buy the 77 acres of land surrounding the college and would pay a price per acre far above the going rate. He also agreed to be responsible for mending all the boundary walls and looking after the woodland, and the college would still have access to Lime Walk.'

The sale went ahead, raising £167,000 plus the maintenance agreement. The money was immediately placed in an endowment fund which it was hoped would cover the maintenance needs of the college for the next decade. It was, as Hilda Jones said, 'a very happy ending to my more than twenty years at the college'.

Educationally, the college was fully living up to its promise. The programme of studies was imaginatively ahead of students' expectations and the lecturers the college was able to attract were of very high calibre. Art, crafts, drama and music courses were always oversubscribed, the college being fully booked for almost every course. Members' complaints, such as they were, were almost all concerned with the difficulty of getting course places. And as always, for every project completed there was another one waiting in the wings.

Hilda retired in 1980. Her farewell party, attended by all the lecturers who had taken courses over the years, together with college friends and

Nimble fingers fashion a fabric box.

staff, coincided with a course on the music of New York, so she really did go out with a swing.

But one of the many disasters waiting to happen occurred when new government fire regulations came into operation. These ruined numerous small hotels up and down the country and many establishments catering for substantial numbers of people were brought to their knees. For a while it looked as if Denman too had received its coup de grace; the cost of the work necessary to meet the new safety standards would be astronomical.

National Council, urgently convened, listened, appalled, as the figures were laid before them. £500,000 was estimated as the minimum amount needed to rewire and repair the premises adequately and to bring in all the fire precautions necessary for a building accommodating so many people.

Financial advisers sternly put the case for closing down the college, selling the house and using the money to run educational activities of one kind or another in various parts of the country, none of them on a permanent basis. Members from the Federations rallied to put the counter-argument: how could anyone even consider closing something which meant so much to all the WIs? Braver women, in much harder times, had conceived the idea of their own educational centre, bought and established it, furnished and funded it: the present generation of members was determined not to let it die. A new fund would have to be raised. A vote was taken; to sell, or not to sell? The answer was loud and clear: not to sell; no, no, no!

Below right: Working in peaceful harmony together.
Below: The finest of petit point.

How to raise the money? National proposed that professional fund-raisers who knew what they were about should be engaged. 'No,' said Executive member Lyndsay Hacket-Pain, also a member of the finance committee, who had listened in disbelief. 'Any professional fund-raiser is going to take a percentage to do the job. How can you ask for money and then give so much of it away?' There was an obvious response to that: 'Then you do it, Lyndsay'.

'Yes,' she said. 'I will, but not for £500,000. If we're going to raise money it will have to pay for the work and then leave a fund for subsequent maintenance. It has to be a million.'

The vote for Denman's future had not been unanimous, ten of the seventy Federations opposed its retention. In announcing the creation of the fighting fund Lyndsay wrote to all the Federations, including the dissident ten. Their response was positive; since the decision to save Denman had been democratically arrived at, then of course, they would support it wholeheartedly. Nothing is more characteristic of the WI spirit.

Wood-turning is as keenly followed as more conventionally feminine crafts.

Each Federation had a target and kept a record. 'We almost lost it!' (meaning Denman) records one Federation. 'We raised over £9,000 towards our £10,000 target. We consciously relaxed a little towards the end because the quite unforeseen generosity of firms and individuals outside the WI meant that the million was achieved in record time, enough to carry out all the improvements and invest for future needs.'

It wasn't quite as simple as that. 'Raising the first £750,000 was easy,' says Lyndsay Hacket-Pain, 'but the last quarter of a million was hard graft. Still, helped by putting all the money into high interest accounts as it came in, and rates were very high then, it grew all the time.'

'...raising the first £750,000 was easy, but the last quarter of a million was hard graft...'

But more potent than the highest of interest rates was the determination of members themselves. 'Once they got going it was incredible; they had sales, made and raffled quilts and other craft products, had balls, picnics, and concerts. They took the money to the bank in wheelbarrows.'

Individual members made gifts. One gave her brass bed: 'We needed a new bed so we got the one then sold the other and gave the money to Denman.' Those who had it to spare gave jewellery. 'We had a diamond necklace sent in. It was wonderful, the response.'

Can the 'Buy a brick for Denman' campaign, instituted in 1992 and still continuing, be necessary after such a magnificent effort? The two are entirely compatible. The maintenance fund meets repairs and

"Do you think this colour goes here?" Expert and not so expert consult.

'...the "bricks" ... enable more students than ever to benefit from the Denman experience...'

costs, the 'bricks' are building new residential units and an Activity Hall to enable more students than ever to benefit from the Denman experience.

For some years after the retirement of Hilda Jones there was a series of short-term Principals; Executive exerted strong control over both college management and educational policy. Student numbers began to fall: an urgent need to re-establish a coherent plan led to the appointment in 1989 of an experienced educationalist as Principal. The right person for the job turned out to be a man.

Graham Jones had been an Education Officer in Buckinghamshire and Hampshire. Well-versed in dealing with staffing, course design and purely educational matters, he was also a politician, accustomed to dealing with government officials, examining boards and all the tiresome details that overtake good teachers when they cross the boundary between classroom and management. He could also cope with Executive committees.

'...greater order combined with a more coherent sense of purpose...'

Executive committees are by their very nature part of a voluntary structure, mostly amateur and certainly temporary. An educational policy should be devised and carried through by educationalists. What emerged in a very short time was greater order combined with a more coherent sense of purpose.

The college had in fact been a tremendous success in terms of what it offered and delivered to students. Now it was time to get back to what the members of the Nineties wanted, and to devise courses to meet their needs

To the individual WI, Denman is the focus of change and growth, the full flowering of their achievement. Having raised the money for its purchase, upkeep and development, they naturally want to see it with their own eyes. The college is now open for students the year round except over Christmas; 348 days in total.

While it would be disruptive to a teaching establishment to have visitors traipsing through all the time, visits by Federations and groups are nevertheless frequent, open days are catered for in the timetable, and festivals every few years with Denman as the venue are actively encouraged and well-attended.

As Denman is owned by the WI, members are proprietorial, but so are the students who are paying for tuition. The college is primarily for residential students, and a careful balance is maintained between potentially conflicting interests.

Educationally, the college has advanced to meet the changing times. It is now self-financing in its day-to-day running. Its income is from student fees just as the National Federation's income is from members' subscriptions. For this reason college policy has to be student-led. Under the terms of its foundation Denman College is a trust. Since the NFWI became a corporate body in 1991, the college trustees are now the NFWI Executive Committee. The Denman Trust sets goals and targets; Principal and staff promote policies and implement them.

Forward policy is now to achieve recognition of competence; recognition that work done within the WI, to the standards it has imposed upon itself, has a currency outside the WI. Since accreditation is needed for outside work, forms of assessment have to be devised and new criteria applied.

The college has worked with accrediting bodies such as the Royal Society of Arts, the Open University and the National Extension College by means of which students can gain qualifications for personal fulfillment as much as, if not more than, for vocational reasons. From the beginning it has been possible to gain WI certificates which would qualify successful entrants to teach at WIs, group meetings and even in the public sector. Now there are more and more clearly defined objectives to be attained.

A five-year plan for the college was launched in 1993. The first priority was to increase its residential capacity so that more students could be

Above: Découpage, cutting out the layers.

Below: Découpage, an almost finished picture.

housed. The Croft, an older part of the college outbuildings which had provided student rooms since 1952, was coming to the end of its life. Replacing it with more and better cottages would greatly improve accommodation and make it possible to put on more courses for the members.

There is something particularly rewarding about building programmes. The ceremonial laying of foundation stones is fun. For the new cottages, Mabel Lukes, a long serving member of staff, and Susan Stockley, the then National Chairman, were joined by students and some invited guests. Also, there is the opening ceremony to enjoy, but, most of all, the knowledge that you are contributing something solid, something that will endure as part of a worthwhile institution, is among the most satisfying of human activities.

'...the knowledge that you are contributing something solid, something that will endure as part of a worthwhile institution, is among the most satisfying of human activities...'

This time, when the cottages were completed in 1993, there was to be no Royal opening, or rather, the WI would call upon its own royalty. One cottage was to be opened by the godmother of the college, Lady Brunner herself. A near neighbour, she is still a frequent visitor and takes a close interest in all of Denman's activities. Nor have her 90 years dimmed her perception in the least. She spoke of her pride – our pride – 'that Denman College has survived, not easily, let it be said, but with tenacity of purpose. It is significant that it has held its own when Adult Education Colleges are pretty beleaguered. Succeeding generations ... have kept alive the vital sense of ability to achieve an ideal that motivated ... those who pioneered the college in difficult but somehow less threatening times than those we face today'.

'...the vital sense of ability to achieve an ideal that motivated ... those who pioneered the college in difficult but somehow less threatening times...'

The second cottage – they were named Beech and Willow – was opened by the Marchioness of Anglesey, who first joined the National Executive at a mere 29 when Lady Brunner was chairman. Stressing the value of being 'flexible and ready for a change', Lady Anglesey expressed her disagreement with author and art critic John Ruskin, who had claimed that he was 'now 51 years old and little likely to change my mind on any important subject unless through weakness of age'. The thousands of WI members who pass through Denman every year certainly don't hold to that stuffy belief.

The Golden Jubilee celebrations in 1998 will hopefully see the culmination of the five-year plan to extend physical facilities as well as to advance in educational terms. Every year 6,000 members take a residential course at Denman and a further 1,500 come on day visits and every three years up to 15,000 members attend one of the week long Festivals. The WI philosophy of personal growth through learning is central to the personality of the movement: Denman is central to the philosophy of personal growth.

6: LEADING LADIES

THE end of hostilities in 1945 brought the end of another era; the retirement of Lady Denman. Although she had had thirty years of relatively autocratic if benevolent rule, she nevertheless preached and applied principles that were firmly democratic. It was she who ensured that no dominant individual could overrule the wishes of the majority; she who set in place the procedure for changing leaders constitutionally, smoothly and without offence, whether at the village hall or the Federation meeting or National Executive.

Electing a national leader is a two or even threefold process. The chairman of the NFWI Executive committee must be able to preside over a group of women who have been elected because they have demonstrated ability in their own Federations, and, in many cases, been Federation chairmen themselves.

All have ideas and opinions; the first among them must have diplomatic talents and marked authority. The leader of the whole movement should additionally have presence and personality. She must come across to the membership as someone to whom they can easily relate, but whom they also esteem, hold in respect, and even love. Ideally she should have the vision to inspire. Since she represents the largest voluntary organization for women in the country she will be required to talk on their behalf to government and public bodies, speak out for them on many a public platform, act on their behalf and in their best

Above left to right: Lady Denman, first Chairman for 30 years. Countess of Albemarle, DBE, NFWI Chairman 1946–1951. Lady Brunner, DBE, JP, Chairman 1951–1956.

Mrs Pike, Chairman 1961–1966.

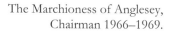

The Marchioness of Anglesey,
Chairman 1966–1969.

interests as and when the need arises, and answer to them for the consequences. To the media she is the WI. Last but certainly not least, she is the employer and controller of a large staff and must maintain a balance between this secretariat, who are semi-permanent, and an Executive which is in a constant process of change. She is now furthermore the chairman of a limited company with an annual budget of some £2,500,000 and fixed assets of the same approximate value. There is also the major additional property of Denman College, of which she and her Executive are trustees on behalf of the members who are its actual owners.

Every aspect of WI training and experience ensures, time after time, that the right persons move steadily to the fore from village WI through County Federation committees to national level. The majority of them, after leaving office, will continue to serve society in one field of activity or another.

The elected chairmen from 1946 to 1969 were all but one titled and all 'establishment' women. From a stratum of society which had access to people of influence, they could, often through personal contact, make the needs of the movement known where it most mattered. They were also characterised by youthful vigour. The Countess of Albemarle held the reins when she was still in her thirties, as did Lady Brunner. Lady Dyer, Gabrielle Pyke and the Marchioness of Anglesey had none of them reached middle age when they took the chair in their turn. Lady Brunner was an actress, Lady Dyer an academic, Gabrielle Pyke ex-MI5 and the daughter of a bishop, while Lady Anglesey was the daughter of a novelist and a playwright. There was never a conscious gap between the leaders and those they led. In the committee rooms at county or national level, all rose to officer status by democratic election. Social position, standard of education and knowledge of the world may have fitted them better for leadership, in their time, than the majority of their fellow members but they earned their position by ability.

Lady Dyer, JP,
Chairman 1956–1961.

7: BRAVE NEW WORLD
1945–1970

WITH commendable foresight, Kent-West Kent Federation anticipated the end of the war by celebrating with a music festival planned for and actually taking place in May, 1945. They could call on 26 choirs to take part, although they had had to struggle to find sufficient copies of the music: there were no photocopying machines in those days, and not much of anything else except hope. Determination and optimism triumphed over shortages of food, fuel, clothing and even space.

Many servicemen and women had married and started families before finding homes to live in. Overcrowded houses were commonplace as parents shared accommodation with their children and a new postwar generation. Affordable housing is in short supply again in 1994, but in the exhausted years that followed final victory everyone was in the same boat until the new housing they had been promised became available.

A mandate in 1943 had pledged the movement 'to consider ways and means by which the WI can help in the postwar relief in Europe'. In 1944 sewing and knitting parties incredibly found the means to make 25,000 garments for distribution in Europe before the end of 1945. It was thus a relief from the continual grind of 'making do' and doing good to to be able to turn to the less utilitarian aspects of life. Hands which had knitted tirelessly for the war effort also produced exhibitions of fine craftsmanship, though even these showpiece products were often given to those in need. But there was another project in hand. NFWI Executive now had a mandate to find a property that

'...determination and optimism triumphed over shortages of food, fuel, clothing and even space...'

WI Exhibition in the Lord Mayor's Show, 1947 – through the City.

Dr. Inna Kryzhanovskaya from
Russia and Lady Anglesey.

could become a college, and the hunt was on. So was the task of raising the money needed; £60,000 for starters. It was a tremendous sum for those hard times.

Money-raising is a way of life in the WI. Each Institute is self-supporting and the need of the WIs to earn their keep is something that has a unifying effect. Members of the WI become ingenious and imaginative in finding ways of exercising their talents, practising their skills, entertaining themselves or the community, and making a little profit on the side at the same time.

'...ingenious and imaginative in finding ways of exercising their talents...'

The Wiltshire Federation, as an example among many Federations, recently gave each of its WIs £5 with the challenge to earn a profit within a given time. Aldbourne WI turned their five pound 'talent' into £1005 over one winter, so it is not surprising that raising a national fund for the movement's own college was not considered to be an insurmountable obstacle.

In any case, in the immediate postwar period there was a nationwide determination to provide more educational facilities. Young people returning from the armed forces had a lot of catching up to do; many had been compelled to abandon educational courses while others never even began them. In the WI, too, many women whose education had stopped short of their aspirations found the idea of a place of learning of their own irresistible, though there was perhaps some anxiety that in attempting to create one they might be biting off a large and unchewable mouthful.

'...many women whose education had stopped short of their aspirations found the idea of a place of learning of their own irresistible...'

In the meantime Lady Denman was succeeded by Lady Albemarle. Her vice chairman, Lady Brunner, was the person who inspired the Annual General Meeting with her vision of a country house as a college. Warm and welcoming, it would be both a centre of learning and a haven in which members would find respite from domestic pressures for a few days while pursuing personal interests in the company of their own kind.

'...centre of learning and a haven in which members would find respite from domestic pressures...'

As to housing in general, postwar WI resolutions stressed the need not to overlook rural needs. There were still many village houses with privies rather than fairies at the bottom of the garden. Rural transport, water supplies and main drainage were other deficiencies. Wartime queues continued into peacetime and materially worsened. Countrywomen knew they would remain at the back of the queue unless they kept up the pressure.

Throughout the land individual WIs kept themselves very thoroughly informed on conditions in their own home territory. A questionnaire, *Our Village*, examining the conditions and needs of rural communities, was completed by almost every WI. The summarised findings were published in 1950.

Busy years for the WI, but they still found time to hang up their aprons, and put their minds and their voices to more joyous use. Recognising that a united burst of song would lift the spirit, the NFWI Executive not only arranged a Combined Festival of the Arts in 1946 but commissioned a work from Ralph Vaughan Williams specially for women's voices. *Folk Songs for the Four Seasons* was scheduled for 1950. Many hours of rehearsal were spent on something which could be learned by separate choirs all over the country before they came to London to sing it together. Reinforced by the London Symphony

'...a united burst of song would lift the spirit...'

A WI choir raising hearts and voices in Marcham village church, during a Denman Festival.

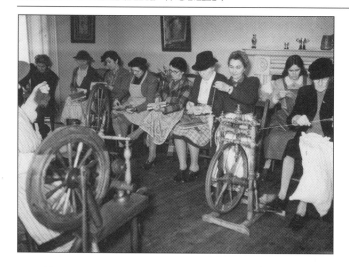

Above: A WI spinning school at Ashford, East Kent.
Above right: Leatherwork class at Flamstead WI, Hertfordshire.

Below: Southerndown, Glamorgan, Resolution 1958 (see page 88) "... to improve inadequate sewage systems ... to prevent pollution of watercourses and seashores."

Orchestra under the baton of Sir Adrian Boult, nearly 3000 voices soared to the great roof of the Royal Albert Hall, 920 in the choir and a further 2000 in the auditorium. A work which can be divided into manageable parts for separate rehearsal, then assembled as a whole in a central place, is an ideal vehicle for a large, enthusiastic but scattered body of participants. It involves the active co-operation of the maximum number of people, the interest and support of many more, and a consequent sense of triumph when the parts come successfully together in the eventual combined performance.

Singing festivals are one such vehicle, pageants are another, and pageants are the very stuff of county events. At agricultural shows, where the WI is always a presence, they are a natural crowd puller. Large outdoor spaces present an opportunity for hundreds of performers to be involved.

Pat Bond of Norfolk is an acknowledged pageant queen. Starting as a co-producer in 1968, she has since organised no less than five of her own. 'Of course, it's the members who are so wonderful; they'll tackle anything, or we couldn't even begin.' They come from WIs all over the Federation. Each pageant has portrayed the life of the district, featuring local history whenever a colourful connection could be made. One took place in the grounds of the hall where Henry VIII first set eyes on Anne Boleyn, so that incident naturally figured largely in the show.

Another pageant involved scores of flappers shimmying and doing the Charleston across the grass, illustrating the Twenties in a historical parade. All have focused on aspects of women's life through the ages; all have involved casts of hundreds; all have performed to hundreds more. The development of the creative arts accelerated. *Home and Country,* the WI's magazine, had been underwritten by its first editor and the movement's first playwright, Alice Williams, from the proceeds of her successful play *Britannia*. Many other members put their varying writing talents to use to produce plays which could be performed by small groups of women of similarly varied talents. The search for good plays for women is unending and anything of merit can be assured of a growing number of performances as the word spreads. Kent-West Kent held a Kentish Cavalcade in 1950 with a cast of no less than 800 members, but then, they were working to a well-established tradition; they produced their first spectacle in 1924.

Every Federation marks its significant events with some form of celebration. Variety shows figure frequently in a style that is quickly recognizable. Whether called Extravaganzas, Follies, Old Time Music Hall or Frolics, the formula of mixed music, monologues or duologues, sketches, skits and playlets follows a familiar pattern. Standards may vary but the practice is a welcome perennial.

'...standards may vary but the practice is a welcome perennial...'

After the success of the singing festival, playwright Robert Giddings was commissioned to write a work for a drama festival. He wrote *Out of This Wood*, a group of five plays with related themes, which were offered to WIs throughout the country to choose for competitive production. Each WI could enter one play. Then followed a process of elimination from Federation to region, with the finalists performing all five plays in London in 1956.

The drama festival was followed by a playwriting competition which drew 393 entries, and the winning script was performed. Producers' and actors' courses at Denman College were oversubscribed and standards of production and performance rose markedly. Support and encouragement are still available for beginners, with no lack of opportunity to practice. Every Federation has its music and drama sub-committees, and combined entertainments feature in every Federation programme, from village pantomimes to reviews. In 1994 even an opera,

Below left: British mothers watch a simple demonstration at the Birmingham Welfare Centre, as part of the maternity and child welfare schemes of 1945.
Below: Demonstrating in a farmhouse kitchen was a far cry from the clinical setting of today's domestic economy centres.

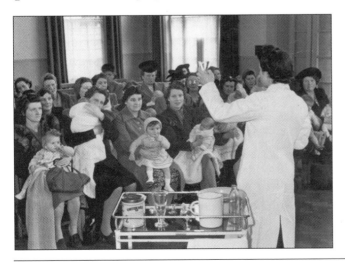

Right: General view of the Jam Centre room at Merenworth WI, Kent.

appropriately based on Louisa May Alcott's *Little Women*, was written and performed by members in Cornwall.

And resolutions from the WIs continued to show their will to fight. The beach of Southerndown in Glamorganshire is one of the finest in the country. Children brought up in the area learned to swim in the murky waters of the Bristol channel, unable to admire their toes through even a few inches of water. The discharge of untreated sewage into the sea added to the hazards.

It was Southerndown WI, in 1958, who began the fight against the pollution of our seas and rivers. Their resolution brought a surge of support not only from other coastal towns and villages but also from all members who flock down to the sea whenever the sun shines. Today there is a new sewage treatment plant on the River Ogmore and the waters at Southerndown are clear enough for toes to be seen.

Below: The village midwife does her rounds. The WI battled for better care for childbirth in the country.

Building for peace was as much in the mind as those early post-war rejoicings. The WI pledged support for the newly created United Nations as they had done for the League of Nations before the war. They strongly supported their own Associated Countrywomen of the World, and through them sought and later won consultative status at the assemblies of the world's decision-makers. In the programmes of individual WIs international topics were as high on the agenda as planning and housing.

Profound changes were taking place in British society. Peace might have come, but the war had ended with the dropping of the first nuclear bombs; a whole generation was growing up in the knowledge that they still lived in dangerous and highly unstable times. In 1962 the WI, at its Annual General Meeting, urged an end to the testing of nuclear devices in the atmosphere.

Bob Dylan was the voice of the new generation, warning us all that new answers to old questions were "Blowin in the Wind", and "The times they are a-changin". But while the young tended to mock their square elders and preached peace their mothers practised it and its arts.

In 1960 NFWI handed over the £5,200 collected by WIs to the United Kingdom committee for World Refugee Year. Counties adopted refugees and their families and continued to do so for many years. And having pledged support for the Freedom from Hunger campaign in 1961, the movement drew up plans for quite specific projects, 'not for temporary help but to reinforce specific schemes for agricultural programmes to enable underdeveloped countries to increase their food production, raise nutritional standards and market surplus produce.' These are the principles which still apply in ACWW.

'...to enable underdeveloped countries to increase their food production, raise nutritional standards and market surplus produce...'

In 1965 the movement celebrated its Golden Jubilee with dinners, parties and, of course, speeches. In Surrey, county president Barbara Paine saluted 'the young women of today, setting out with the vote in one hand and the Pill in the other'.

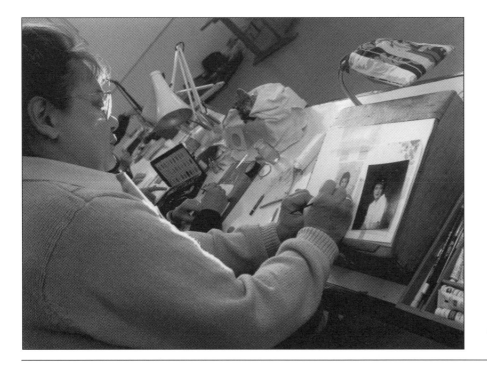

A Denman student portrait painting from photographs.

'...valuable historical records...'

In the same year the WIs once again recorded the state of affairs in their respective communities. The resulting scrapbooks are valuable historical records, lovingly summarized by Paul Jennings in his book, *The Living Village*, and also drawn upon in *Village Voices*. Many are now kept in county archives.

The WI was achieving an increasingly high profile. The drama festivals and musical performances, together with displays at such showcase occasions as the Royal Show, the Olympia Ideal Home Exhibition and the Dairy Show, were all attracting attention. Of course, that was part of the idea, in addition to giving members an incentive to display old skills and practise new ones. Both Federations and National are always searching for ways to stimulate fresh thinking. But the general public was already finding many aspects of country life increasingly attractive. The after-effects of the war had receded. New housing was springing up, much of it in semi-rural areas. The age of mass car ownership had arrived, making town-dwellers increasingly mobile.

'...the idea of living in the country, or at any rate on the edge of it, had growing appeal...'

Entire new towns were being built in various parts of the country, the theory being to have a mix of people from every walk of life. The idea of living in the country, or at any rate on the edge of it, had growing appeal. One developer in Surrey approached the Federation when a new estate was being completed, with an offer to pay the costs of a hall for whatever inaugural meeting was necessary to start a WI there, 'to help create a community'.

New arrivals meant new WI members, often more worldly-wise, with new ideas and different talents to mingle and marry with the tried and the true. Bearing in mind that the WI was originally intended for rural women, the rule that a WI may only be formed where the population is less than 4,000 originally made sense. There were now many thriving WIs where the 4,000 mark had long been passed. And women in other communities which did not meet the rule were clamouring to come in. As town came to meet country, country members proved more than able to hold their own. Accepting the reality of the situation, the rule was rescinded.

'...the WIs flourished with exuberance...'

On another sector of the public relations front, new ways of keeping the WI's name before existing and potential new members were pursued with imagination and élan. The WIs flourished with exuberance. They entertained parties of elderly people from nearby towns, who loved a day in the country, with tea, entertainment and a posy of fresh flowers to take home. In Kent they had teams of cricketers, in Suffolk too. 'We played the men every August Monday. They always played with police truncheons instead of bats, so we always won,' say West Bergholt. Many ran their own classes, taken by more skilled members.

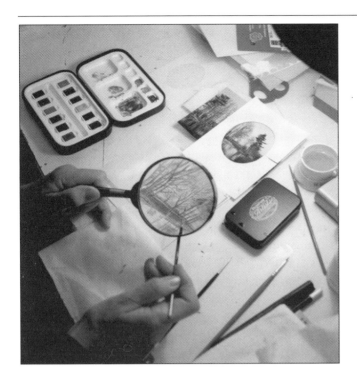

These extra curricular activities provided both instruction and a lively social time, as they still do in many WIs. In Holmwood, Surrey, one keen dressmaking student wheeled her sewing machine to class in a barrow.

Above left: Painting miniatures at Denman.
Above: Learning to frame the results.

A competition to depict Country Feasts and Festivals was seized on with enthusiasm. Carol singers, a picnic on Box Hill based on the one in Jane Austen's *Emma*, boar's head processions, country weddings, christenings and harvest suppers: idealized versions of country life proliferated. Each Federation had its winning entries; only the choicest reached Olympia but it was all a stimulus to creativity enjoyed enormously by everyone who participated at every stage of the competition. The following year saw the first National Art Exhibition staged in London. The fine arts had become more prominent: every painting course at Denman was oversubscribed. Federations were already holding their own exhibitions. The quality of workmanship was often all but professional, as had already been evidenced in presentation books given to Lady Denman, and to our present Queen and fellow WI member as a wedding present.

'...the quality of workmanship was often all but professional...'

The degree of dedication was demonstrated by one artist member painting on the edge of a river. When a sudden gust of wind snatched her masterpiece and carried it out into the water, she instantly stripped to her underwear and waded in to rescue it, to the general applause of her WI art group. The Marchioness of Anglesey was an enthusiast for the arts. The NFWI had established itself as a patron by commissioning

Painting outdoors offers a more direct contact with nature, in spite of possible hazards.

'...just think, we went from our tiny village in Westmorland to sing in the Albert Hall!...'

Out of This Wood. A new project was even more ambitious. In flamboyant spirit the National Federation commissioned composer Malcolm Williamson and librettist Ursula Vaughan Williams to write a work which would tax all the creative and organizational skills of the WI.

The Brilliant and the Dark, composed by Malcolm Williamson and performed in 1969, related 'the woman's view of history', ranging back and forth through the centuries, contrasting the tragedies of widowhood, war, injustice and poverty with the jubilation of British women's achievement, individually and collectively; the brilliant contrasted with the dark. The work was planned so that it could be sung as a grand event with a cast of hundreds plus soloists and orchestra, or in sections in a village hall, with piano accompaniment. The staging was splendid: costumes made by WI 'skilled labour' were created from materials given for the event by Courtaulds.

'Blue and turquoise for the sea sequence, white and black for the suffering abbesses, rootless after the Reformation, brilliant greens for the pre-Raphaelite Summer Dance, airy pastels for the Spring Dance, stark red and white for the Wars of the Roses. Such lavish, flamboyant dresses have not been seen in town for many a day,' said *The Financial Times*.

Staged in the Albert Hall, 150 actors and dancers from WIs in Hertfordshire and East Sussex performed in dance and mime to the singing of a thousand-strong choir accompanied by the English Chamber Orchestra conducted by Marcus Dodd. Every Federation was involved; choirs chosen by competition to take part travelled to London. 'Just think, we went from our tiny village in Westmorland to sing in the Albert Hall! It was terribly exciting. But when we were rehearsing there was a percussionist in the orchestra just below us enjoying a cigarette. People weren't so fussy about smoking in those days as we are now but it annoyed us, I can tell you. Not good for our voices!'

The sewing, too, was shared among the Federations. 'I remember stitching and ironing many of the costumes. There were these lovely fabrics given by Courtaulds, it was a joy to do.' The Federations who contributed their members and their energy also staged their own performances, maybe only of sections of the whole, but it gave the local members a chance to see what they had all been working for. Exhilarated by success, some of the singers wanted to continue. A WI national choir was planned which could be available for concerts of high standard with a well-known conductor. The resulting choir enormously enjoyed working with Antony Hopkins and developed a great esprit de corps. The Avalon Singers, as they called themselves, gave a public concert in 1975 in the Purcell Room of the Royal Festival Hall.

8: THE AGE OF THE 'EXTRA ORDINARY' WOMEN 1970–1994

BY the late Sixties improved educational opportunities for women began to yield dividends. Certainly they contributed to the change in social climate which through the Sixties and Seventies resulted in a steadily growing pool of talent for the running of the movement.

Women still, in the main, brought up their own children, with time left to use their creative skills and mental energies on behalf of a voluntary organisation. The WI provided plenty of stimulus for those prepared to look beyond their village boundaries and accept a challenge.

Top: Alderman Mrs Pat Jacob JP, Gloucestershire Federation (1974–77).
Above: Mrs Patricia Batty-Shaw CBE, JP, Norfolk Federation (1977–81).
Left: Queen Elizabeth the Queen Mother with Miss Sylvia Gray CBE, Oxfordshire Federation (1969–74).

Below: Mrs Anne Harris CBE, Kent-West Kent Federation (1981–85).
Bottom: Mrs Elizabeth Southey, Surrey Federation (1994–).
Bottom Centre: Mrs Agnes Salter, Oxfordshire Federation (1985–88).
Bottom right: Mrs Jean Varnam OBE, JP, Nottingham Federation (1988–91).
Right: Past NFWI Chairmen's Meeting with NFWI Chairman Elizabeth Southey: 1994. l to r: Anne Harris, Patricia Batty-Shaw, Elizabeth Southey, Lady Brunner, Jean Varnam, Susan Stockley.

Increased prosperity provided an opportunity, willingly accepted, to "put a bit back in the kitty", in the words of a Cheshire member. Most WIs had keen elections for committee, a choice of possible presidents. Federations could take their pick of possible sub-committee members. National committee members could be drawn from any part of the country. There was a plethora of talent to draw upon.

The NFWI chairmen who followed Lady Anglesey were ordinary women only in the sense that they lacked titles. Nevertheless they were leaders with qualities honed in the WI. Not all travelled by the same path; each was unique.

9: CHANGING BOUNDARIES, CROSSING FRONTIERS 1970–1976

THE WIs were thriving and exuberant. They ran their own affairs competently; they knew the annual subscription was inadequate to pay their way, but they could earn the difference and the earning was part of the challenge and part of the fun of WI life. But the movement as a whole was less securely based. Sylvia Gray, who succeeded in 1969, claimed to be the first chairman to have truly 'risen from the ranks'. Certainly she was very different from her predecessors in her areas of expertise. 'Sylvia was like a liner sailing along with us little boats following behind', says former treasurer Kate Foss. They were hardly little boats; she had some very able people with her, but she knew exactly where she wanted to go, so they were happy to go along with her.

Just as everyone at the top is first and foremost a WI member with the WI at the back of her, Sylvia Gray was a member of Burford WI in Oxfordshire. There she owned and ran two hotels and a shop. A self-made businesswoman, she ran training schools for her staff, all women. A WI member since her late 'teens, she also played a strong part in local government. But it was her business skills which were to the fore when she looked at the national finances.

Good stewardship and calm oversight are the watchword for county executives in their capacity as houseowners and keepers of the purse, according to the Buckinghamshire Federation. How much more should this apply to the National Federation, with the responsibility of managing the affairs of an organization of independently-minded units, shiningly generous towards the unfortunate or a major appeal, notoriously tight-fisted when it comes to their own affairs?

'...good stewardship and calm oversight are the watchword for county executives...'

The WI subscription alone had never been sufficient to support adequately the three arms of the movement: WI, Federation and National. Yet it was the only assured form of income. True, there were government grants for educational work and the Carnegie Trust was generous for specific projects, but there was no guarantee that such funding would continue. True, WI markets were profitable and donated profits to the National kitty, but that had to pay for the Markets adviser and schools for producers. *Home and Country* was a splendid contributor, but still, it was not a satisfactory or a comfortable state of affairs.

Lady Denman had set up an endowment fund in 1920 to form the basis of 'large reserves', but time overtook their value. The annual subscription fixed by the membership at their AGM had remained the

The Coat of Arms of the National Federation of Women's Institutes (see page 101).

The lion crest, symbolising both England and Wales, is depicted in red and gold to pick up the colours of the four lions on the arms of the Prince of Wales for his Principality. Lions are traditionally associated with courage and determination; this one also holds a distaff – that long-standing symbol of woman-hood – and so makes this a symbol to be reckoned with!

The heron represents the country-side and the elements of water, air and earth by which it lives. These herons are distinguished from other heron supporters by standing in clumps of reedmace.

The motto: well, we think it speaks for itself! The WI Badge reflects the main motif of the arms, and is con-tained within a ring – symbolising unity and perpetuity.

NB Because the Grant of Arms was made to NFWI, they then became the property of National, and it is therefore not permissible for the Arms to be reproduced other than with the permission of NFWI Executive.

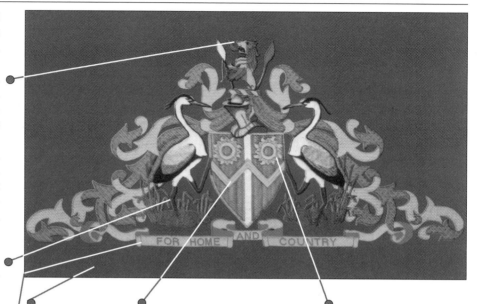

Green was chosen as the basic colour for the shield, to represent the country.

Heraldic convention requires that the metals gold and silver be placed on a colour, and vice versa. Letters are not usually incorporated but, rather conveniently, one ancient symbol, the bar dancetty, looks like a W; another, the pallet, looks like an I!. These two were used, in gold and silver respectively, to form our initial.

The two golden, pierced suns have a double meaning: symbols of life and vitality, but also (and more cunningly!) as a pun on the arms of Pearson, which was the maiden name of Lady Denman, founder Chairman.

same from 1917 to 1939. Subsequent increases were very small. In 1963 National appealed for a reasonable increase: it was not approved.

The Queen Canutes stood stubbornly on the shore and watched the tide rise, rescued time and again with money raised from festivals, concerts, exhibitions and voluntary quotas. An appeal for an invest-ment fund of £500,000 was launched. By 1969 the appeal had reached its target, but inflation was already beginning to erode the value of the fund. The next treasurer, Kate Foss of Westmorland, with Pat Jacob of Gloucestershire as chairman, had stark figures before her and was the first treasurer to have to face the AGM and announce a deficit in the accounts. It had already been necessary to make a withdrawal from the reserves to bridge the gap, but the rate of outgoings made it clear that the National Federation of Women's Institutes would be bankrupt in the foreseeable future.

In times of financial crisis there are very few options open: earn more, cut back, 'get by with a little help from your friends'. The WIs were

Lady Brunner plants a commemorative tree at the Silver Jubilee of Denman College, September 1973.

sternly for cutting back, though their members, most of them house-wives, knew that there is a limit to the number of things on which one can economize.

Pruning was thorough and continuous but over-pruning can kill the tree. Earn more – a realistic increase in the membership fee – was the one option members seemed determined to resist. A resolution brought by the Surrey Executive to allow the NFWI Executive in Consultative Council, rather than members in General Meeting, to fix the amount of the subscription was finally agreed. So the mechanism to raise subscriptions was in place. But the three options had still to be applied.

'...pruning was thorough and continuous but over-pruning can kill the tree...'

In the meantime there was pressure from members up and down the country for a fundamental change in the constitution. There had been an influx of members who had married during or immediately after the war. These were energetic 30 to 40 year-olds who, having brought up their children to manageable ages, had more time for themselves. Actively concerned with the great social issues of the day, topics which were being openly discussed on radio and television, they wanted to be part of the great debates. One of the rules in the constitution forbade discussion of anything 'of a party-political or sectarian nature'.

It became obvious that it would be impossible to influence parliamentary opinion without being political. Many of the resolutions coming forward from the WIs reflected the new mood, but the constitution, drawn up to safeguard village communities from dissension, ruled out such vital topics as, for instance, comprehensive education and family planning.

WIs had long held carol services or thanksgiving services in cathedrals and minsters, blithely ignoring the 'non-sectarian' character of their movement. The question to be answered now was whether the movement was sufficiently intelligent and sophisticated to pursue its aims by political means while remaining outside the party political arena.

In 1971 a resolution to rescind the 'no discussion rule' was proposed by the NFWI Executive Committee. The debate was long and fierce but Chairman Sylvia Gray guided firmly. All points of view were heard, from the fearful to the forward-thinking. When the vote was taken it was decisively in favour of change. The wording of the new rule re-affirmed that 'the WI is non-party political and non-sectarian', with all shades of opinion respected, but the rule would not be so interpreted as to prohibit discussion on matters of public concern. As Lady Albemarle had asked in earlier days, 'Why have we been educating ourselves for over fifty years if we can't now tackle difficult problems?' And tackle them they did.

'...why have we been educating ourselves for over fifty years if we can't now tackle difficult problems?...'

Until the rules were changed it would have been unthinkable for the WI to discuss birth control. Yet no subject could have greater importance for women. Outside WI meetings the provision of family planning advice was widely discussed; Lady Denman had been a pioneer supporter of the family planning lobby and of the Marie Stopes clinics.

Gwen Davies, a social worker in the Isle of Anglesey, was well aware of the hardship endured by many women who, through ignorance, were obliged to bear more children than their health or family budget could stand. In addition, the number of unwanted pregnancies of teenage, unmarried girls was a perennial problem. For those with money, access to medical advice was easily available. For those who really needed it, where pregnancy could be a real disaster, clinics were available in large cities but in rural areas there was nothing.

'...clinics were available in large cities but in rural areas there was nothing...'

Prompted by Gwen Davies, Anglesey Federation executive committee submitted a resolution asking that family planning advice should be made freely available. The resolution was vigorously discussed in every WI. They all knew of cases of unwanted pregnancies, of sad abortions, of tragedies of illegitimate children, less accepted then than now. The resolution was passed overwhelmingly; today family planning is part of the health service and has been since 1974.

Resolutions reflect the way in which WIs respond to what is happening in the world. In 1969 the first men landed on the moon. The awesomeness of the event seemed to emphasize the vulnerability of our own small planet and concern for the environment and conservation assumed greater urgency. Ideas for a competition to illustrate Our Green and Pleasant Land started to buzz around the collective WI brain. Little Llanover WI in Gwent still cherish the signboard from their entry as a reminder of their communal pride when it won a place in the final exhibition at Olympia.

Other national and world events tested feminine resourcefulness. A series of national strikes at home forced a few changes of habit. With bakers on strike, many members turned to *The WI Book of Yeast Cookery* and made their own bread, some for the first time. Having found the making therapeutic and the result delicious, they seldom went back to the bought product.

'...national and world events tested feminine resourcefulness...'

In order to cope with a postal strike, many counties devised a system of personal delivery by sub-committee members from Federation office to strategic centres around the Federation for WI collection. The system – or some variant of it – christened Percival Post in Surrey after its instigator, is still in operation.

When a power cut threatened a group lunch, one enterprising cook remembered a talk on hay box cookery and devised her own. Using expanded polystyrene as insulation in place of hay, she brought her casserole to the right temperature on a camping stove, popped the contraption into the car and drove off, with the improvised hay box completing the cooking successfully during the journey.

But more contentious issues demanded collective decisions and a firm guiding hand. In 1974 county boundaries were changed by Parliament in the greatest reorganization of local government since 1888. Only ten of the forty-five English counties and one out of the thirteen Welsh counties were unaffected. Cumberland, Westmorland, Huntingdonshire and Rutland (as independent authorities) were abolished. Such synthetic creations as Avon and Humberside made their debut to what it would be polite to call mixed feelings.

'...more contentious issues demanded collective decisions and a firm guiding hand...'

A great deal of discussion on these proposals had already taken place in the country. Counties arranged information days and made representations to Government at the Green and White Paper stages. Many of them were receiving grants or assistance from their local education authorities, so any change in those authorities meant financial upheaval for the WI Federations too. The NFWI realized that the Federation boundaries too would have to change, but it was something much easier to say than to do. New Federations would have to be formed, others divided. Some WIs would be in one Federation, their friends and

*'...outbreaks of downright
rebellion...'*

neighbours in another. Not surprisingly, there were great outbursts of emotion; little pleasure and much pain, not to mention outbreaks of downright rebellion.

The principles of what was to be done were agreed in the time of Sylvia Gray. It was the next chairman, Pat Jacob, who had to carry them through with Kate Foss, National treasurer, in support. In 1975 they began the unenviable task, splitting off Avon from Somerset and Gloucestershire, bringing Humberside into existence, launching West Midlands and Cleveland and splitting Cumbria into two Federations. Only the Federations of Wales derived a little pleasure from the proceedings, having fun in choosing new names to go with new county names or bringing back names from the past. That's why we have Dyfed-Caredigion, Dyfed-Caerfyddin and Dyfed-Pembrokeshire. One of the difficulties was financial: each new Federation needed funds, and the only solution lay in prising some of their funds from existing Federations. No one likes parting with money and the Federations were no exception to the rule.

Some Federations had become involved more directly with administrative changes; they protested to the government as villages found control of their schools passing from one local education authority to another. WIs affected often turned to their public affairs committee for advice. Small wonder that a resolution from the National Federation asked the government to consider giving financial support to those protesting against proposed plans when they had to attend public enquiries. But these were large issues affecting many people. Sometimes WIs take up cases of more personal significance. They could turn from changes forced on the whole to simple problems concerning individuals.

*'...sometimes WIs take up cases of
more personal significance...'*

In the village of Rowledge in Surrey an elderly couple were faced with a heartbreaking situation. Both were in poor health; both needed medical treatment; neither was in a fit state to make hospital visits. An obvious solution, as they were terrified of separation, would be to admit them both together to hospital or nursing home.

But there was just one problem. In 1969 hospital beds were available but not for a couple. When they were sufficiently recovered to be moved it was equally difficult to find a home prepared to take a married couple. Rowledge WI took up the case. Could they bring a resolution to the Annual General Meeting and get the weight of the NFWI behind it to urge for accommodation for married couples to be made available if the need arose? Rowledge first consulted their Consultative Council representative. They discussed the wording and were closely questioned about the problem. Was this case unique? Research would have to be done through social services, Age Concern, nursing homes and hospitals to see if other cases had arisen and what the outcome had been.

In the course of exhaustive enquiries questions went to the Welsh Board of Health and on to hospitals throughout the principality. Among the answers received: 'Have no records of any cases but, as you have brought the possibility to our attention, will immediately issue instructions that in such a case the couple should not be separated if it is medically possible to treat them in the same or nearby wards.'

The resolution was listed for possible inclusion on the agenda of the AGM. It was the job of the council representative to put the case forward to the Consultative Council, who had the final say. The subject was emotive, although the actual cases were few; the resolution was chosen. At the Albert Hall an amendment reduced the original wording, addressed to 'hospitals and old peoples' homes' simply to 'old peoples' homes'. It was considered that medical problems could make the first part unworkable. Yet, as we have seen, by simply bringing the resolution and asking questions the problem had already been brought to the attention of a significant part of the health service.

'...simply by bringing resolutions and asking questions, problems are brought to significant attention...'

But there was celebration too. Another anniversary, the National Federation Diamond Jubilee was due in 1975. To celebrate it a history of the WI was commissioned under the sponsorship of the Carnegie Trust. The book, eventually published in 1977, was *Jam and Jerusalem*. Its author, Simon Goodenough, later became even more closely associated with the WI, as a member of the Board of WI Books.

In another commemoration, Kay Shearer, National vice chairman, undertook a special project. When each village WI holds its monthly meeting a cloth is put on the table along with flowers and the president's bell or gavel. National did likewise, but its cloth, originally a fine example of WI craftsmanship, was showing marked signs of age and wear. Why not commemorate the jubilee with a new cloth worthy of the movement's dignity? And how much better if it had something special in the way of design to grace it? NFWI consulted the College of Arms: could the WI have its own coat of arms? Richmond Herald at Arms said yes, of course; anyone who could establish appropriate credentials could have a coat of arms if they were willing to pay for it. The credentials of the National Federation of Women's Institutes were impeccable and the College of Arms duly created the design (see page 96).

'...the College of Arms duly created the design...'

The Royal College of Needlework translated the design in terms of embroidery. The work of creating the cloth was then undertaken by a Kent-West Kent team under the supervision of Nancy Kimmins, a noted craftswoman and instructor to the county. The cloth in all its magnificence now appears at all the movement's official public meetings.

One further step remained. A member attending a meeting of local authority representatives noted the wide range of chains of office worn. She wrote to National suggesting that the WI's chairman too should have a public chain of office worthy of her official dignity as the representative of a movement of national standing and high reputation. No sooner said than done: the new coat of arms was reproduced on a Chairman's brooch first worn by Anne Harris and subsequently by her successors up to the present day.

'...different events, different responses...'

Different events, different responses; conferences and consultation are appropriate to change but sometimes there was a chance 'to inform' and have fun too. The country had made a stride forward into a different world by becoming part of the European Community. Counties put on exhibitions, concerts, colourful days of information and entertainment. Choirs sang the songs of our neighbours from across the water; wine tasting and cookery demonstrations concentrated on Italian, French and German dishes; talks on any corner of Europe figured in WI programmes. A good time was had by most and even one sub-committee member when asked to portray Luxembourg in an exhibition depicting Community members, was saved from despair when they won the Eurovision song contest the week before the show, providing her with just a bit more material with which to fill her stand.

'...welcome to Europe certainly added spice to life...'

Welcome to Europe certainly added spice to life. The WIs and Federations, eyes firmly on their own environment, grasped the opportunity to 'plant a tree in seventy-three'. Some even made it a wood. All over the country planting ceremonies ensured that England and Wales would remain green and pleasant into the future. But even the WI needed a little help from our friends'. In the Seventies any hope of further government assistance, even for educational projects, was dim. Over the many years since the WI came into existence charitable organizations have been generous in their support for specific projects. The Carnegie Trust, a staunch friend, has been an active supporter since the very first years of the WI's existence. In 1970, for example, it financed the Town and Country project and in 1977 underwrote the production of the WI history, *Jam and Jerusalem*. Whenever a particularly ambitious plan is put forward, similar sponsors are sought to bear some of the cost.

Organizations and businesses recognize the advantage of supporting worthwhile activities undertaken by sympathetic allies or potential customers. It keeps them in the public eye. Durham have a highly appropriate sponsor in Madeira Threads, who, as their name implies, make materials for embroidery and craftwork. They backed the Northern Arts and Crafts show at Beamish College, Durham, to mark the Durham Federation's 75th anniversary. All the northern counties seem to have a fairy godmother in the form of Taylors Tea, who intelligently advertise themselves by setting a competitive puzzle in the various county newsletters every month, with a prize from the celebrated Betty's in Harrogate. Look what they're missing in the south! But for the 75th anniversary of the movement, Tetley's, undaunted by a total of 8,600 institutes, obliged on the grand scale, providing the tea for every celebratory teaparty. A possible 350,000 people could have said, 'Thank you, Tetley,' as they raised their cups.

No company with an eye to the main chance is going to miss a good thing in the sponsoring of so much purchasing power, but 'We are extremely careful in our choice of sponsors,' said Jean Varnam. 'They mustn't offend the sensibilities of members or the principles of the movement.' So tobacco companies are hardly suitable, nor breweries perhaps, but our partners in enterprise have included National Express Travel, Safeway, British Home Stores, Vauxhall Motors and the National Westminster Bank.

'...no company with an eye to the main chance is going to miss a good thing in the sponsoring of so much purchasing power...'

The Federations of Wales have a very generous annual grant from the Welsh Office in recognition of their valuable contribution to Welsh rural life and their language, and in turn undertake many projects on behalf of the Welsh Board of Health, the Countryside Council, the Royal Life Saving Society and the Welsh Consumer Council.

When Denman College sought to equip new teaching rooms and, later, for their next project, the new Home Economics Centre, they first 'let it be known' that they were doing so. The gifts poured in: gas and electricity suppliers, manufacturers of cookers, mixers, dishwashers, microwave ovens; every manner of domestic appliance. Not surprisingly they were happy to have an opportunity to show off their products to 'students' who became potential customers as soon as they returned home.

'...happy to have an opportunity to show off their products to 'students' who became potential customers as soon as they returned home...'

Since 1990 the NFWI has been a limited company. By law, a meeting of delegates from every one of the nearly 9,000 Institutes must be held every three years. The only suitable venue is the National Exhibition Centre in Birmingham. This triennial meeting is a costly undertaking, as AGMs always have been. To help fund it, and to provide something of an exhibition for the members before and after the official business, space is leased to suitable organizations and individuals in the exhibition hall next to the conference facilities. The WI itself takes centre stage with displays on Denman College, *Home and Country*, WI Books, the Federations of Wales and WI Markets. The National Farmers'

Penny Kitchen, editor of *Home and Country,* right. Nora Arnold, NFWI Executive liaison Officer, centre. The stand depicts the 75th Anniversary of *Home and Country,* from manual typewriter to computers, from the first editor, Alice Williams, to the 1990s.

'...NFWI is seen as an important force in the community...'

Union has a stand, as do the Council for the Protection of Rural England, the National Extension College, the Women's National Commission, the Sports Council, the National Trust and COPUS, the Committee on the Understanding of Science. Also present are most of the high street banks.

It may give a 'commercial' feeling to the occasion or make it resemble an agricultural show, but it is a useful reminder of the fact that the NFWI is seen as an important force in the community. And it certainly makes the mounting of a meeting essential to the proper functioning of the movement less expensive than it otherwise would be. Yet another example of good housekeeping.

A delegate to the 1994 triennial reported to her WI, 'They all seemed to be talking about money.' When the National treasurer makes her financial report to members – who are in this case also her shareholders – it is vital that she should talk about money: indeed, it's impossible that she should talk about anything else. If she has been a wise and prudent manager she will have good news to report and members should listen intently, for the future welfare of their movement depends upon that prudence.

10: OUR WORLD, OUR FUTURE
The WI and the International Community

THE WI has never been inward-looking. In their very earliest pro-grammes there is evidence that they were interested in the problems of the world. For many centuries this island itself has been the centre of a family of countries, from settlements to empire to commonwealth. Every WI has overseas connections of some kind or other. International relations really come in two parts. There are the relations of the NFWI with other countries; people constantly calling on us, our paying visits to other countries to see how things are run; and then the way in which the affairs of the rest of the world impinge upon the health and interests of the WI.

You can get the picture from WI resolutions. From the 1920s there have been many concerning international affairs, particularly in such matters as the general search for peace. Societies of rural women sprang up all over the world after the formation of the first one in Canada. We in this country were by no means the only ones. We weren't even the first; we followed the Belgians.

In each of these countries the leaders were in contact with each other, formally and informally, and what was at first a fairly informal network grew. Everyone's aspirations were the same; the advancement of rural women through education, and the improvement of the quality of rural life. People would come to Britain and say, 'Can you tell us how to start a WI movement?' Sometimes members from the NFWI would go out and help to start movements elsewhere. Visitors passing through London constantly called at headquarters to learn how such a society was run and to visit WIs if their time allowed it.

At the same time our own WI frequently covered international themes. Each Federation has lists of speakers available for programme plan-ners, and a review of these reveals the breadth of interest. Buckinghamshire alone, for example, has ninety-one talks available on international themes. Naturally, many more contacts were made during the 1939-45 war. Overseas forces were stationed here, overseas relationships were kept up, while our own people who served abroad replicated the situation elsewhere. A positive spider's web of links and contacts was woven in this way across the globe.

In 1927 a resolution brought by Berkshire Federation urged 'closer co-operation between similar groups of women overseas with a view to mutual assistance and understanding', but by the time that resolution

'...the WI has never been inward-looking. In their very earliest pro-grammes they were interested in the problems of the world...'

'...societies of rural women sprang up all over the world after the formation of the first one in Canada...'

'...everyone's aspirations were the same; the advancement of rural women through education, and the improvement of the quality of rural life...'

'...a positive spider's web of links and contacts was woven in this way across the globe...'

was brought, Mrs Watt was already back in Canada and herself working to create a more formal connection between all these branches from the original Canadian tree.

'...the redoubtable Mrs Watt had a dream of uniting them all in one huge international society...'

The redoubtable Mrs Watt had a dream of uniting them all in one huge international society. Not everybody was with her on that. All these different societies were developing in different ways, according to the conditions in their particular countries. It was difficult to see how they could become one enormous federation with the same constitution and rules, but Mrs Watt was always looking farther ahead than everyone else.

An international organization already existed. It was the International Council of Women, which the WI had been invited to join. They and other rural women's societies from different countries went for the first time to participate in an international conference in Antwerp in 1929. The NFWI sent a representative, who reported back that the Scottish Rural Women had been represented by a full delegation of three members, as were the Northern Ireland WIs; both of them being member societies.

It gave the NFWI something of a jolt, initially forcing them to conclude that they could not be left out. However, they learned that this conference had been completely dominated by urban topics. All the issues considered were related to the affairs of women in towns and cities; no space was provided for discussing rural affairs.

'...the Associated Countrywomen of the World...'

The concerns of rural women were remarkably basic: such elementary necessities as clean, drinkable water that actually came from a tap, sewage disposal, education, transport, all of which were naturally taken for granted in the towns. The countrywomen went away united. If there were different constitutions and rules in each country, there could not be a federation, but they could certainly associate with each other. The result was the Associated Countrywomen of the World. ACWW was officially formed in Stockholm in 1933. Surprise, surprise: their first chairman was Mrs Alfred Watt. She held that office for fourteen years; in fact until a year before her death.

'...there were enormous advantages in presenting a united front...'

There were enormous advantages in presenting a united front. A large international organization stood a far greater chance than any single national body of making its views heard and its presence felt on the world stage. ACWW can be represented wherever it is likely to count. It has consultative status at the United Nations, where it is a Wingo (a women's international non-governmental organization), one of many non-governmental organizations which are represented at the United Nations.

There are conferences of Wingos, in which ACWW participates. They have a direct voice on bodies concerned with economic and social activities; education, science and culture; children, development programmes, population activities, world health, the environment, world food and the development fund for women. They also have links with commissions on the status of women, social development and human rights, so that, in effect, even the smallest WI in this country has a link with and a voice on almost every aspect of human activity.

ACWW has projects all over the world. It usually works on the order of a five-year plan. In 1994 it had sixty-three different on-going projects in twenty-eight countries. It does not work on the principle of raising money and saying, 'Right, you can have so much to do this.' It has a very firm policy of helping each particular country, in a very specific way, to help itself. It sets up training programmes or provides the means by which people in that country can improve their lives by their own individual effort.

'...in 1994 ACWW had sixty-three different on-going projects in twenty-eight countries ... helping each particular country, in a very specific way, to help itself...'

For instance, in the 1960s, WI markets in our own country supported the establishment of a market in Lesotho. The Lesotho women grew more than they needed for their own purposes and set up an organization to sell the surplus, simultaneously providing for others and making their own lives a little better.

The contribution of the WIs was recognized in 1984, when the Queen of Lesotho went to Denman College to see what women there were doing, and the King of Lesotho visited the 'Life and Leisure' exhibition to receive the final cheque for the project. In other parts of Africa water projects have been set up. There are currently sixteen projects, limited in nature and also limited in time, after which they are monitored to make sure that they continue to function properly. In so many parts of the globe women spend, and in effect waste, a great part of their time in the unproductive task of simply fetching and carrying water.

They have to raise money with their crafts stall. Their teachers are trained, then go back and teach how to produce something which will sell, working on from there. The village associations are always the leaders. Very often these projects are based upon links between countries. To take a specific example, Tongan women were helped by WIs in Victoria in Australia to build new roofs for their kitchens. The roofs of their kitchens were made of dried grass which rotted in the rain. The rain was putting out the cooking stoves. The men refused to help because it was not considered to be men's work. The women were wholly occupied in rearing their families, cooking, and making things which they could sell to tourists who arrived in cruise boats at infrequent but very specific times.

'...the village associations are always the leaders...'

The women of Victoria raised money to help to repair and reinforce the kitchen roofs, the Tongan women themselves also providing part of the cost. The success of the operation was confirmed at a later date when a great hurricane brought down many of the island's houses but left the rebuilt kitchen huts intact.

There were a number of projects in India to set up temporary clinics to detect eye complaints. The projects, run by ACWW, paid for the travel expenses of volunteer doctors, for food, patient accommodation and for advance publicity. The temporary clinics were successful and another eye clinic project was launched in April 1992. In some of the areas covered by the projects there is a superstitious belief that disease is a punishment from God. Now free teaching has introduced basic concepts of hygiene and nutrition that are designed to match limited incomes.

'...now free teaching has introduced basic concepts of hygiene and nutrition that are designed to match limited incomes...'

In South Africa ACWW ran a project to improve the quality of life and self-esteem for thirty women from a particular area in Lesotho. It provided advice on food production and fuel-less cooking, sewing skills, nutrition and health, including information about AIDS. Those attending such classes are always encouraged to share what knowledge and skills they acquire with other groups, in order to create a continuous learning process.

'...classes are always encouraged to share what knowledge and skills they acquire with other groups, in order to create a continuous learning process...'

In Brazil a very big project in partnership with UNICEF has been carried out since 1978 to improve the health and knowledge of young mothers in order to reduce the mortality rate. There is a tremendous illiteracy problem among Brazilian women and the work undertaken there includes the development of literacy. It concentrates particularly on the women of the streets. Prostitution is the only way in which many of them can make a living, increased literacy one of the ways of helping them to escape from it.

Another Brazilian project is that of 'the nut breakers of Babaka'. Clusters of Brazil nuts, 12 to 15 at a time, grow wild inside very hard capsules roughly six inches across. The women cut the capsules open with an axe, not, as one might expect, by bringing the axe down on the nut but by holding the axe, blade uppermost, between their toes, and bringing the outer shell down on it. It is a task requiring great skill and judgement.

'...what was needed to increase their 'income' was a donkey, twenty axes, and eight oil lamps...'

The nuts are ground to extract oil. A great many nuts go to make a kilo of oil, which in turn will buy a box of matches or a quantity of sugar. Nut oil, then, is the women's currency, and what was needed to increase their 'income' was a donkey, twenty axes, and eight oil lamps to enable them to go on working after dark.

Lyndsay Hacket-Pain, former member of NFWI Executive and elected World president of ACWW in 1995, is an intrepid traveller. Going round the world at her own expense, she plans her trips to cover ACWW projects, then visits individual WIs and WI groups to talk about what she has seen. When WIs offer help for the nut breakers she suggests 'an ear of a donkey? A leg? A tail?' She has priced every single part! To buy a whole 'kit' – axes, lamps, donkey – costs £430: so far she has raised £2,500 for the Babaka women – nearly six donkeys and sets of tools – ACWW working in harness with UNICEF on such projects.

In northern Greece seminars concentrating on the environment and healthy living have been very succesful. In Swaziland they were building latrines and since the girls' school had only one communal tap they needed a reliable clean water supply for the school and for the teachers' dwellings. With the help of a Canadian ground survey team they drilled a successful water hole, ACWW providing the money to buy and install a submersible pump and a water storage tank.

An outside lavatory is a typical facility for rural areas and many have been funded and provided as part of safe water projects. Safe water is always a primary self-help project, the more so since maternity units, even when available, are usually dependent upon clean local water. Twenty-one different islands in the Fiji group have been assisted in this way.

'...twenty-one different islands in the Fiji group have been assisted...'

In South Africa, in the Transvaal, more than 800 women attended information sessions and workshops staged for them by South African WIs but funded by ACWW. To raise money for women's projects in Natal a member from Gloucestershire, Caroline Carroll, did a sponsored walk which covered all the WIs in Gloucestershire. In calling on each WI she not only raised money from her sponsors but also accepted gifts of materials, which she took with her when she went to Natal to present the cheque.

Women are the principal labour force in food production in many parts of the world and ACWW's present theme is 'Women feed the world'. The central office of ACWW is in London, which is the easiest place for everybody to get to, but since delegates have to travel from all over the world, they do meet every three years in a different country. But it has to be a country where members from every ACWW society are welcome; in other words, somewhere where they will be admitted regardless of race, creed or colour. They could not, until recently, for example, meet in South Africa.

'...women are the principal labour force in food production in many parts of the world ... "Women feed the world"...'

The NFWI belongs to ACWW and has a very strong presence, members of Executive always attending evey triennial. The National chairman was a delegate to the twentieth triennial conference, held at

The Hague in 1992. On that occasion delegates representing 9,000,000 women from sixty-three countries were welcomed by HM Queen Beatrix of the Netherlands. Among the many vital topics reported, discussed or covered by resolutions were global warming and the greenhouse effect, the conservation of genetic resources in the world's plant life, biochemical engineering as it affects small farmers – women cultivators in particular – and the creation of wholesome environments for women and children.

'...the creation of wholesome environments for women and children...'

WI Federations can be a constituent society in ACWW, a corresponding society or an associate society, according to the size of the membership fee they pay. According to that status they may send a delegation of five, three or one to the triennial conference. Many WI members are members in their own right and can attend any conference if they wish to.

In 1971, at the thirteenth triennial, which was in Norway, the then vice-chairman of NFWI, Olive Farquharson, was elected world president. In 1992 Avon, Devon, Glamorgan, North Yorkshire East, Nottinghamshire, Kent-West Kent and Wiltshire Federations were represented, but so, in their own right, were WIs from Butts Brow in East Sussex, Hutton Bonville of Essex, St David's from Dyfed and Winchcombe of Gloucestershire.

But that is not the only international activity NFWI is involved in. In its own right it may go out, as it did in Malaya, through Viola Williams, to help start up a WI movement. Quite remarkable visits are undertaken: for example Gabrielle Pyke, when she was chairman, had an invitation from the Soviet Union to go out and explain how a women's organization ran.

'...quite remarkable visits are undertaken...'

She went at a time when moving freely around that country and meeting people was out of the question. After she had been taken round various factories and co-operatives she said she was not willing to do any more trips of that kind; she wanted to meet rural women. Miraculously she did manage to do just that, rather to the surprise of the British government, who didn't even know she was there. In consequence, a woman member of the Soviet praesidium came over to visit women's organizations in this country in the late Sixties and attended an Annual General Meeting of the NFWI.

'...a woman member of the Soviet praesidium attended an Annual General Meeting of the NFWI...'

Apart from projects around the world supported by ACWW on the basis of the five-year plan, the WI itself will also spring into action when crises come about. A notable example occurred in 1961, when the South Atlantic island of Tristan da Cunha was evacuated after a massive volcanic eruption. When the islanders returned in 1963 they were helped by WIs, who raised money to replace some of what they

Toys being packed for Romania (Isle of Man Federation). Women's responses are generous and immediate to knowledge of other women's hardship.

had been obliged to leave behind. In addition, while the islanders were in this country, the WI arranged agricultural training and information programmes for them so that they went back knowledgeable in new practices and techniques.

More recently, the emergence of Eastern European countries from behind the Iron Curtain has brought a full realization of some of the terrible things that had happened in them. Since the fall of the regime in Romania many organizations from Great Britain have sent teams over to assist in the process of recovery. In 1990 such a mission was organized in the Doncaster area and two South Yorkshire WI members became involved.

'...two South Yorkshire members became involved in a mission sent over to assist in the process of recovery in Romania...'

'...the best action that could be taken was to teach the women to organize themselves to make use of the practical help that WIs here could offer...'

One, Marjorie Ward of Bawtrey WI, participated through a church group but there was such a rush of volunteers that others were chosen by ballot. Catherine Watson of High Levels WI was among this party, backed by the South Yorkshire Federation, who raised money to provide some of the items that a preliminary assessment had shown were needed. It was decided that the best action that could be taken was to teach the women to organize themselves to make use of the practical help that WIs here could offer. Once again they were backed by the South Yorkshire Federation, who raised money to pay expenses and fund the purchase of a van to transport both team and equipment.

Marjorie and Catherine made several trips, realising that their best contribution lay in reaching out to the Romanian women and helping them to unite, organize, and help themselves. Through their efforts four Romanian women came to Britain in 1993 to visit NFWI and see for themselves how to run a women's organization. Under the wing of the South Yorkshire Federation they also spent two weeks visiting, and seeing something of the countryside.

In 1994 a party of WI volunteer teachers, demonstrators and helpers went out, each paying their own expenses, to run a 'mini-Denman' for groups of women in Transylvania. This too was organized by South Yorkshire but there were so many volunteers from all over the country that they were again chosen on the basis of their skills and by ballot. Basic funding for the scheme came from the charity Know How. The

A visit to NFWI Headquarters by Romanian women, 1993, welcomed by NFWI Executive members Mary Thomas and Ann Lindon.

events which led to the collapse of the Soviet Union have resulted in many former member societies coming back into ACWW. Estonia, for example, was a founding member but was locked away behind the Iron Curtain for over half a century.

The last European conference, in 1993, was held in Estonia, whose members were so delighted to be able to restore their contact with the rest of the world's women's organizations that they particularly asked for the conference to take place in their country. They chose a castle large enough to accommodate all the delegates; the world president of ACWW, Mrs Valerie Fisher, went with her deputy the night before to get a first impression of the facilities. The castle, quite superb from the exterior, proved to be somewhat primitive inside and the two visitors found themselves involved in cleaning bathrooms and lavatories. They also discovered that hot water was on a Tuesdays and Fridays basis. In general the living conditions proved to be those the Estonians themselves had had to accept for the entire period of the occupation, no bad thing for more fortunate delegates to experience and one which, needless to say, they adapted to with their usual versatility.

'...the 1993 European Conference in Estonia...'

Nevertheless the Estonian conference was a great success, and an extra bonus from such meetings is that news of the way in which womanly solidarity can be brought into play travels from one part of the world to another. When asked, 'What can we best give?' the answer is invariably, 'Training, training and more training.' Mrs Fisher, the ACWW president, went straight from Estonia to the United States. Without asking for a thing, she got an immediate response from women's organizations in Colorado and Texas, the American women undertaking to fund Estonian projects.

'...when asked, "What can we best give?" the answer is invariably, "Training, training and more training."...'

The European Area president, currently Yrsa Berner of Norway, arranged a further conference of the Eastern European countries to identify means of getting them back on their feet. Among the participants were Romania, Greece, Poland, Hungary and the Baltic countries. This meeting, held in Prague, was also funded by Know How and a grant from the European Union.

It is generally recognized that the quickest and most cost-effective way of improving life in the world's rural areas is the direct funding of women-based projects. One of the most important parts of ACWW's work is in self-help projects, building on whatever are the traditional values of family life in a particular area, and developing community projects, providing access to education, training and self-sufficiency

'...the quickest and most cost-effective way of improving life in the world's rural areas is the direct funding of women-based projects...'

Sixty-three projects in twenty-three countries were supported between 1991 and 1994, covering areas such as health, family care, safe water, sustainable agriculture, leadership training and community development. In the Solomon Islands training in sewing and home economics is helping to combat urban drift. One of the projects in Transvaal is familiar enough to WIs in this country, since it consists of courses in public speaking and meeting procedures. It need hardly be said that in the new political climate in South Africa such skills are likely to be of major importance.

A question that might understandably arise is, 'But how is all this activity funded, since it must be enormously expensive?' Apart from raising money for specific projects the greatest expense is simply the cost of travelling; paying for people to go to conferences. The world is divided into a large number of areas and each area has its own conference.

'...the greatest expense is simply the cost of travelling...'

Take the Gilbert and Ellice Islands, for example; a conference in their area might well be in Australia. Delegates might have to start weeks beforehand even to get there and would need to be funded for their journey as well as their necessary expenses after they arrive. The money is raised in a very simple way. Mrs Godfrey Drage, a Welsh member, realised that annual subscriptions from societies and individual members would never provide sufficient money. She had the brilliant idea of every member providing one penny a year.

'...she had the brilliant idea of every member providing one penny a year...'

In practice, of course, it isn't always a penny, but the smallest unit in the local currency. First named 'Pennies for Friendship', it is now broadly known as 'Coins for Friendship', since every WI in every country voluntarily raises money in this way. 'Coins for Friendship' represents the greater part – 75% – of ACWW's income many WIs and Federations raise a great deal more.

'..."Coins for Friendship"...'

An example is Kent-West Kent, which by raising £5,000 has funded a complete ACWW project unaided. And just as South Yorkshire backed the Romanian projects, other Federations carried out a project for the Windward Islands some years ago. It was the rule in the Windwards that small children could not go completely nude to school. WIs, through ACWW, started a fund to send sewing materials to the Windwards, making up packages, each of which contained sufficient for a garment for one child, plus cotton, buttons and zips, together with sewing machines, scissors, needles and thimbles. The Canadian Save the Children fund administered the scheme in the islands.

Among the many changes which have affected people's lives in the British Isles, the most far-reaching took place in the 1970s. In 1972 the British government signed the Treaty of Brussels. In 1975 a referendum was held to see whether the British people were still sure that they wanted to be part of the then European Community. The result was a two-to-one majority in favour of continuing membership. At that point NFWI chairman Patricia Batty-Shaw and general secretary Anne Ballard found themselves facing a completely new situation.

Relations between the NFWI and the British government, whose decisions affect everyone's daily life, have always been cordial; the NFWI lets them know what its concerns are and the government listens. Now there was a new and different group of decision-makers in Brussels who could equally affect any and every aspect of the lives of members. How could the NFWI have access to them?

In 1977 a group of Executive members went to Brussels on a fact-finding mission. They wanted representation and they found the means. As a result of their meetings with officials and with members of organizations from other member countries, a new body came into being; COFACE, the Confederation of Family Organizations in the European Community.

'...they wanted representation and they found the means...'

Fiona Ross is currently the NFWI representative on COFACE's administrative council, on which the United Kingdom as a whole has four members. The council meets three times a year in Brussels to consider existing or pending legislation on issues affecting the people and interests of the member nations they represent. A further meeting takes place between these representatives and DG5, which is a group of civil servants from various countries who are actually engaged in drafting the legislation.

As meetings take place at the actual planning stage, it is possible to have direct and immediate effect on legislation, and certainly easier than trying to bring about changes in legislation already passed, a very tortuous process. 'It's more informal dealing with Brussels than Whitehall,' said Fiona Ross. 'Much more direct. You can say, "No, rural women don't want that." At the last meeting we considered rights to parental leave (from work after childbirth), European directives on education, and the youth programme. DG5 deals with social affairs.

'...it's more informal dealing with Brussels than Whitehall ... much more direct...'

'Since Maastricht there has been a flood of legislation and initiatives to improve life. We're in a position to work with voluntary organizations in other countries. We can exploit the system. The NFWI, for example, can draw upon European Union money for projects we want to undertake. The Welsh Federations have been particularly successful in this. They've already undertaken health projects with the Welsh Board of Health, and are investigating the possibility of more.'

But to most individual WIs, making international links means connecting with a similar group in another country, making pen-friends,

'...to most WIs, making international links means connecting with a similar group in another country...'

exchanging life stories, news and descriptions of their daily lives. WIs can be linked to any country in the ACWW network through a special contact.

In this way Holmwood in Surrey formed a link with a group in Trondheim, Norway. Letters and greetings were exchanged. Holmwood staged a Norwegian day for their Leith Hill group, learned Norwegian dances, baked a Kranskake. Two of their Norwegian friends came to visit; later, through an arrangement with Holmwood, a link daughter, Vigdis, arrived as an au pair. After her return to Norway Vigdis married and had a son.

In Surrey one of the 'special WIs', St Ebbas, a hospital for the mentally subnormal, heard about the WI's overseas links. 'I wish we could have a link,' someone at the hospital said, 'but I don't suppose there's anyone like us.' The Holmwood president heard about it, remembered that Vigdis's son was similarly handicapped, and wrote a letter. Through this contact a link was established between St Ebbas and a hospital in Norway, and they exchanged drawings, postcards and stories about themselves. On another level the staff at both hospitals could exchange ideas and experience on the treatment of those in their care. So a genuine advance in international understanding came about in a small but very human and personal way: opportunities to open doors, opportunities to walk through them.

'...a genuine advance in international understanding came about in a small but very human and personal way...'

Indian children delight in their new jumpers knitted by the WI. These children earn their living by rag picking and balloon selling.

11: LEARNING TO BLOSSOM FORTH

The Very 'Special Institutes'

MANY new resolutions brought to General Meetings urge government action, but there are fewer on which WIs themselves can take action. When they can act, they do. In 1957 Devon Federation urged WIs to stretch out a hand to the mentally ill. An earlier mandate introduced by Essex had called for WIs to concern themselves with the education and welfare of the mentally handicapped. Triggered by Devon, Federations contacted their local psychiatric hospitals, or were, in some cases, approached by them. In 1958 the first WI was formed in a psychiatric hospital in Cambridgeshire.

'...Devon Federation urged WIs to stretch out a hand to the mentally ill...'

Two more followed in 1960, in Somerset and Cheshire, a fourth a year later in Yorkshire, and four the following year in Derbyshire, Durham, Hereford and Worcestershire, and Dyfed-Caredigion. The pattern was now established: Federation VCOs and executives knew how they would work. Normally members of the hospital staff were the guides on the committees, helped by members of the hospital League of Friends. Members of nearby WIs came as voluntary helpers and VCOs attended.

Patients gained from contact with the outside world, recovering confidence, slowly learning to communicate and regain an interest in life.

By 1968 there were fifteen such WIs all in psychiatric hospitals where patients were being treated for mental illnesses from which they were expected to recover. Participation in a group activity such as a WI meeting, on a social basis, was therapeutic, the more so as the fellowship demonstrated would also be available in the community to which patients would be returning. But catering for the temporarily ill and the permanently handicapped raised two different sets of problems. On the one hand there was the expectation of a return to normal life in the community. On the other was the question as to how those in institutions could usefully participate in normal WI activities.

'...the question as to how those in institutions could usefully participate in normal WI activities...'

In 1968 a hospital psychologist approached the National Federation with a view to having a WI in Royal Earlswood, a Surrey hospital for the mentally handicapped. There was little doubt that contact with people outside the hospital hierarchy would be a breath of fresh air for the patients. Much discussion ensued in and out of the Surrey executive committee and among the VCOs, but after exploratory meetings there was still uneasiness. Could this be a real WI? Could the mentally handicapped genuinely be members?

'...do we apply intelligence tests to all our members?...'

Mrs Kay Shearer, the Surrey county chairman, finally asked a question which went straight to the heart of the matter: 'Can they understand truth, justice, tolerance and fellowship?' Whereupon someone else promptly raised another pertinent point: 'Do we apply intelligence tests to all our members?' It was decided to recommend formation. By 1976 Surrey had seven 'special' WIs, three in psychiatric hospitals, four for the mentally handicapped.

Royal Earlswood ran well for many years. They had outside speakers on crafts, flowers, animals, faraway places. They had singing afternoons, country dancing. They discussed resolutions, and even brought one to a Federation meeting themselves. It was a matter on which the patients had felt deeply: a child had been found dead, trapped in an abandoned refrigerator.

'...we have lovely shells on the shore in Anglesey...'

One of their older members, a long-stay patient, said that all refrigerators should have their doors removed before being scrapped, to avoid future accidents. It was a very sensible idea and the resolution was passed, raising the question of why such an intelligent and caring member was a long-stay patient. Lady Angelsey, then National chairman, paid them a visit. As she was leaving she said, 'We have lovely shells on the shore in Anglesey. I'll get you some so that you can use them to decorate boxes.'

'...if you want something done, ask a busy person, especially if she's a WI member...'

The night before the next consultative council, when a national chairman invariably has a great many things on her mind, Lady Anglesey phoned Paddy Martin, the Royal Earlswood VCO. 'I've got those shells,' she said. 'Don't forget to pick them up.' At the reception desk was a large bag full of shells gathered by Lady Angelsey and her children specially for the members. 'If you want something done, ask a busy person, especially if she's a WI member,' as Clwyd-Denbigh say.

'...a Home for Exceptional People...'

This is the story of just one of fifteen similar Institutes formed by 1976 in hospitals for the mentally handicapped all over the country. Paddy Martin prefers the American term for such a hospital: a 'Home for Exceptional People'.

Was the exercise worthwhile? 'No one could help noticing the changes,' said psychologist Mrs Cortazzi, 'both in the patients and the staff. They (the patients) so obviously enjoyed it. They learned to be beautiful. They blossomed forth. Up to then the hospital staff couldn't help thinking of them as patients, then the WI came along and they were accepted as people.'

It would have been easier to invite patients as visitors to WIs, to visit them in hospital, to entertain them, take them gifts, bake them cakes. It was far more difficult to bring them into the WI family, treat them as ordinary members and create or restore self-respect and pride in achievement.

In 1972, Susan North, welfare officer at Calderstone Hospital in Lancashire, invited the WI in. The admirably named Standfast WI, formed as a result, only closed in 1994. 'We like to think that the WI helped these women to cope with everyday social situations when they returned to the community,' said Ms North. 'They had invitations to visit other Institutes, educational days, parties, outings ... we always felt we were an integral part of the WI movement.'

'...the WI helped these women to cope with everyday social situations when they returned to the community...'

Subscriptions for helpers from other WIs, and payment of affiliation fees, gave organization sub-committees and the NFWI Executive administrative headaches. The recent creation of 'associate' and 'dual' membership raises wry smiles today among those who pleaded for such adjustments to meet the needs of the 'specials' and were firmly refused. But it is not uncommon for individual WIs to be ahead of their time. As things were, Federations and other WIs were generous, and the NFWI Executive paid subs for three helpers in each 'special'.

As hospital policy changed and the discovery of new drugs made medical treatment more effective, patients' stays in psychiatric hospitals became shorter before they returned to the outside community. WIs for the mentally handicapped which have closed did so as a consequence of changes in policy in dealing with the mentally handicapped, resulting in patients being moved to smaller homes more closely integrated with the community at large, but nearby WIs have maintained contact wherever possible.

'...nearby WIs have maintained contact wherever possible...'

The need for 'special WIs' diminished in the psychiatric hospitals. Those of the handicapped who could be moved to community houses were transferred, those who remained being so severely handicapped as to be unable to participate. The special WIs – sixty-three of them at their peak – ceased to function and were closed in their turn.

There is still one hospital WI in being: St Andrew's in Northamptonshire. Formed twelve years ago, there are approximately twenty members from the hospital and the surrounding area. About half the number are patients, including two committee members. They are patients who are unlikely to be able to return to the outside community but are able to make visits to Federation events or group meetings when these are suitable.

St Andrew's, a psychiatric hospital, also has patients who are acutely ill and in care for short periods, these patients come in as visitors when they are recovering. Recently in the NFWI newsletter the St Andrew's secretary asked a question: 'Is there anyone out there like us?' She had a call from another Federation who were thinking of starting a similar WI in their own local hospital. If they went ahead they would have the moral support of the many WI members who have had contact with such ventures over the years. They would also be assured that they would be bringing a breath of fresh air into the lives of people in great need of it.

Special members from the
St. Ebba's WI

12: POLISHED PERFORMANCES & WIDENING HORIZONS 1977–1981

BY the late Seventies the scale of the WI operation, the quickening pace of life and a changing social climate, all contributed to a faster turn-over at the top. There was an increased workload for women with homes and families to consider, and less assured domestic help. Time away from home demanded skilled juggling. Three years became the average period of office for National chairmen. This placed a greater onus on the NFWI general secretary and staff to ensure vital continuity.

Patricia Batty-Shaw, who succeeded Pat Jacob, came from the Norfolk Federation. A JP, like her predecessor, her WI experience was in orga-nization and international affairs. No elected committee takes over a blank page from its predecessors; the book is already heavily inscribed with projects only partly completed, problems only half solved, processes of change still working their way through the system.

'...no elected committee takes over a blank page from its predecessors...'

One half-solved problem, the boundary changes, was put on the back burner; another, on-going and perpetual, was the financial balancing act between income and expenditure. Aware of the need to build better bridges with the regions, the chairman 'got out and about. It was important to get the feeling of all the members and take their views back to the Executive. In three years I visited almost every county and all the islands, including Sark. It was a very small plane to Sark and someone passed me a slip of paper for the pilot. It said he was going the wrong way. He was! He had to turn around and change course. He didn't know which way he was supposed to go.'

'...it was important to get the feeling of all the members and take their views back to the Executive...'

Not everyone can influence the course of events from an aeroplane, but while there were indeed plans for change in the air there was also a present course to be followed. There were, as always, a number of issues which, though mandated in the previous decade, were still cur-rent policies: active, still to be brought to a satisfactory conclusion. Equal opportunities for women, equal status for women, the status of women in the matters of pensions and social security were all issues demanding much time and attention. So were environmental concerns, from the disposal of nuclear waste to the threat to marine life from pollution. As legislation affecting such issues comes up it is important not only to ensure that women's views are taken into account but to remind those in authority where such views come from.

'...not only to ensure that women's views are taken into account but to remind those in authority where such views come from...'

This is another aspect of WI work; the organization represents a great weight of opinion. Senior civil servants attended NFWI committee meetings on topics of interest to their departments. She was often at the House of Commons, says Mrs Batty-Shaw, and government representatives, including the then cabinet secretary, Robert Armstrong, used to come to AGMs at the Albert Hall.

In the regions they were involved in practical learning. If education involves innovation, exploration and achievement, what better way to enjoy the process than through drama and music?

This was an area in which members could be put to the test, something which would not only involve them in large numbers but invite them to lay their reputations on the line. As a patron of the arts the NFWI had commissioned drama: *Out of This Wood*; music: *Songs of the Four Seasons* and *Early One Morning*; and, in a combination of both, *The Brilliant and the Dark*. Now it was time to give the Institutes their creative head and discover what they could come up with themselves.

'...it was time to give the Institutes their creative head and discover what they could come up with themselves...'

Cherry Vooght, drama adviser to the National Federation, conceived a plan for an ambitious drama festival, to culminate in performances by chosen groups at the world famous Royal Shakespeare Company theatre at Stratford-upon-Avon. The purpose was to highlight the WIs' work in music, speech and drama, to encourage new writing, and to involve as many members as possible. Patron of 'Scene 80: A Festival of Creative Entertainment', was the actor Donald Sinden, who launched the enterprise at a London press conference. His support was not entirely unconnected with the fact that his mother had herself been president of her own village WI. There were seven classes of work in which WIs might test their skills: revue, play, dance, drama and mime, poetry, story-telling, the spoken word in choral speech, and set or costume design. The aim was to illustrate and celebrate the customs and cultural life of as wide a variety as possible of the English and Welsh regions.

'...Scene 80: A Festival of Creative Entertainment...'

There were sixty-two festivals at county level, from which fifty-seven WIs out of 1,300 entrants won certificates of commendation. Regional festivals followed and although the festival was not in itself a competition, selected groups from Berkshire, Buckinghamshire, Cumbria-Westmorland, Devon, Leicestershire-Rutland, Nottinghamshire, Northamptonshire, Clwyd-Denbigh and Gwynnedd-Merioneth travelled to Stratford for a three-day finale.

The 260 members involved were accommodated in houses normally occupied by members of the RSC in Waterside. There they revelled in a heady backstage mixture of greasepaint and glamour. The bonus of glorious summer weather was a not unmixed blessing for Ginty Lance, the festival director, and a perspiring team of helpers. But a packed

'...they revelled in a heady backstage mixture of greasepaint and glamour...'

audience each night provided all that could be desired in the way of enthusiastic support for the occasion, sponsored by Johnson's Wax.

Pat Bond, of Norfolk, produced many magnificent pageant shows.

In the early days of the WI, in 1919, the Consultative Council was set up to establish close links between the National Executive and the Federations, and so each county had a directly elected representative. VCOs and county chairmen also attended. As social meetings they were excellent, bringing a large conference to a different part of the country each autumn, with local WIs also attending some of its sessions. Yet somehow not enough came back to the NFWI Executive, so a new format was proposed. From 1981, a National Council replaced the Consultative Council to channel grass roots feelings from the outlying regions to the centre, and to select the resolutions for the general meeting. The constituent parts were different. Elected county chairmen and treasurers already represented their counties, so why put in anyone else? And VCOs were left out; this was to be the one time when there could be open and uninhibited discussion with no extra listeners. A vital task of the new council would be consultation on the amount of the annual subscription, and in this the views of county treasurers would be especially valuable.

'...as social meetings they were excellent, bringing a large conference to a different part of the country each autumn...'

Meanwhile another source of income had emerged from the Publications sub-committee, which had for some time initiated a steady flow of literature to supply members with information and advice on their wide range of interests. There were 'how to be' booklets covering every aspect of running an organization: how to be a good treasurer, secretary, president, committee member; you name it, there was a leaflet to match. Books written by members were published; *Lotions and Potions*, the *WI Book of Party Recipes*, the *WI Book of Wines and Spirits*, and every one sold well. WI diaries, produced for members by a commercial publisher, were in demand but the profit to the NFWI was relatively small. There was a constant stream of requests from independent publishers for hints, tips and recipes for inclusion in their own books,

'...a steady flow of literature to supply members with information and advice on their wide range of interests...'

The WI Books display stand in the Teaching Centre at Denman College.

'...we wanted to open up opportunities for members to do their own books...then we started to spread our wings...'

'...it was published all over the place and very successful...'

recognizing that the WI were the acknowledged experts in the field. But the WI were not getting any share of the profit. And WI Publications, a subcommittee of the NFWI, could not expand operations without endangering its charitable status.

National treasurer Kate Foss and general secretary Anne Ballard put their heads together, 'Why not', they asked, 'market our expertise ourselves? Why not follow the example of Markets and set up a separate company?' They picked the brains of friends and acquaintances in the publishing world, and in due course National ventured into the field of professional publishing. In 1977 WI Books was launched as a separate company.

The first operation was the sale of 'part books', a set of complementary titles written by members, published separately but forming a complete volume when assembled. They were printed by Macdonald and were not only successful but very profitable, too. WI Books was in business. The National Federation chairman was ex officio chairman of the board, Kate Foss was managing director, two other NFWI Executive members were also directors, together with a paid general manager and representatives of the publishers. 'We wanted to open up opportunities for members to do their own books,' says Kate Foss. 'We did twenty books with Ebury Press, *Cakes and Preserves*, *Good Baking* and so on. We did a series of *Tour of Britain* books with recipes from the Counties and regions. They were very successful.

'Then we started to spread our wings. We had a regional competition for quilts, and they had these lovely quilts on display at Denman. One of the directors saw them and telephoned urgently: 'Come and look at these. We've got to get a book out of these.' It was called *The Complete Book of Patchwork and Quilting*.

'In that year we went to Frankfurt, to the world-famous International Book Fair, and we were chased all over Frankfurt by all the publishers in creation wanting this book. The rights were sold to the United States, Holland, Germany – it was published all over the place and very successful. In the first ten years of operation WI Books made £1,000,000 profit, including the Federation discounts, for the National Federation.'

The project had started with a loan from the parent company, the NFWI itself, which of course had to be repaid, since WI Books is a business and it has to be run as a business. Apart from the benefit to NFWI finances there is also a benefit to the Federations who act as selling agents, since they always have a discount and get part of the net profits; a 'nice little earner' for them too. But there were limitations to what WI Books could achieve and some inherent weaknesses. Its only constant market was the WI itself, and WI Members suffered from the recession as much as anyone. Though WI Books tried hard to extend the range of subjects in its list, its customers preferred to stick with books on cookery and crafts, and they did not go for new titles on 'women's issues'. Handing over all its profits to the NFWI left WI Books with no reserves at a time of economic ebb. The Board acted swiftly to resolve a cash-flow crisis.

Judy Snowdon

The directors all had wide WI experience but decided that they needed to bring in commercial publishing experience. They determined to contract out the day-to-day management of WI Books, not to a large publisher that would swallow up a substantial portion of their profits and prefer its own interests to those of the WI, but to a small company that would be sympathetic to the aims and ways of working of the WI. The contract went in 1991 to Simon Goodenough, author of *Jam and Jerusalem*, who was a familiar friend of the WI, a publisher for twenty years, and who had recently started his own company, Southgate Publishers.

Within two years, WI Books repaid all its loans to the NFWI and is turning in a healthy profit again, to the benefit of the NFWI as a whole. WI Books chairman, Judy Snowdon, also a former Vice-chairman of NFWI, played a leading rôle in steering the company back into profit and giving it a healthy future.

'...WI Books is turning in a healthy profit again, to the benefit of the NFWI as a whole...'

WIs themselves regularly prove their earning capacity with sales of work to keep themselves afloat. Sometimes counties resort to similar means to replenish the coffers. The idea of a joint national effort had always been too daunting.

Nevertheless it was done. In recognition of the Queen's Silver Jubilee members joined forces and contributed to one mammoth sale of craft work held on a floor of Debenhams Oxford Street store in London. The sale of handiwork from pin-cushions to quilts, donated from all over the country, yielded a handsome sum for the Jubilee Fund, a Trust administered by the Prince of Wales.

'...members contributed to one mammoth sale of craft work...'

It is customary for the ladies of the Royal family to call in at the WI pavilion when visiting the Royal Agricultural Show, to see the current exhibition and to chat to members. Following the Craft Fair, it was the Prince who deviated from his usual route and called in to say a personal thank you to all the members there for such a splendid contribution to the Trust.

QUOTES FROM MEMBERS

WHY DO THEY JOIN?

"'I needed an outside interest.' *Janet Foulsham. Hampshire.*

'I was desperate to get out. I wanted to be busy for me.' *Farmer's wife Sheila Goldsworthy, Cornwall.*

'I wanted to be me now and then and not just somebody's wife or mother.' *Barbara Hough, Hampshire.*

'To be part of an organization that got things done.' *Enid Gratton-Guinness, Hertfordshire.*

'Brownies was childish. I wanted something else.' *Aged 12, Durham.*

'I wanted to enter a competition for a sonnet.' *Daphne Clark, Hampshire.*

'We saw all these women coming out of a meeting all laughing and talking. I said to my neighbour, "I don't know who they are but they're having a great time." We found it was the WI. We joined and we had a great time too!' *Rene Jackson, Surrey.*

'To join the quilting class.' *Pauline Peart, Durham.*

'I used to listen to the Archers and vowed if I ever lived in the country I'd join the WI. It intrigued me.' *Pat Smith, North Yorkshire.*

'I was press-ganged into it by my mother-in-law.' *Barbara Gill, Leicestershire.*

'They had a choir which needed new voices.' *Barbara Ware, West Sussex.*

'To have female company.' *Gwyneth H Sinden, Dyfed-Ceredigion.*

'It was expected of me; I wanted to make friends; I was personally invited.' *Patricia Batty-Shaw, Nottinghamshire.*

'To fill a gap after giving up a full and demanding career to have a son.' *Ruth Pascoe, East Kent.*"

"Why do they stay" and other quotes on pages 172, 176 and 186

13: DIVISION AND DISPLAY
1981–1988

ESTABLISHING the National Council was not the only structural change. Wales, with its strong culture and different language, had a Welsh speaking member on the National Executive. There is also a special committee of their Federations which meets regularly to coordinate activities. In 1980, the NFWI approached the Welsh Office – the government department responsible for Welsh affairs – to find out if the WI qualified for a grant to enable them to appoint a secretary and maintain a base in Cardiff which would serve the Welsh committee and give them a meeting place. In view of the fine contribution the WI makes to cultural and rural life in Wales, the answer was, 'Yes, certainly'. With this recognition the Federations in Wales gained a new focus and impetus for their activities.

The Welsh WIs are a mixture of coastal, rural and urban. Their annual exhibitions at the National Eisteddfod, the May Fair at the National Folk Museum, and the Welsh Show are all meticulously staged and attract the crowds. Yet they are absolutely WI, part of the family, but with their distinct national character. Other regions too pride themselves on their differences. The boundary changes had fired resentment and some resistance. All but one change had gone through; the last had still to be faced, and Anne Harris was in the chair.

'...all meticulously staged and attract the crowds ... part of the family, but with their distinct national character...'

West Kent's Anne Harris, in her own words, was 'a very ordinary chairman'. Needless to say, that is a long way from the truth. She had come on to Executive through WI Markets, which in itself makes her somewhat out of the ordinary. It isn't a usual route, even though markets play such a vital part in WI life. Chairmen tend to arrive via the ladder of organization or public affairs committees.

When changes have to be made, people will fight hard for their ideas and point of view, but once a decision has been democratically arrived at they will normally go along with the majority. Over changing the counties the opposition fought hard, and the last to yield was Yorkshire. They did everything to delay, and succeeded for years. But it went through in the end. 'They thank me now' says Anne, 'come up to me at meetings and say, "We're getting along well. It's working".'

'...people will fight hard for their ideas and point of view, but once a decision has been democratically arrived at they will normally go along with the majority...'

Elsie Charlton, a county chairman and a great Yorkshire character, was implacably opposed. There was a period of slight flux, during all this upheaval, over the Great Yorkshire Show. Who was going to run the WI tent? The Federations were in a state of disarray, so the NFWI

Executive stepped in and ran it. It was unthinkable that the WI would not be there.

'It was really hot summer weather. The night before, we went into the WI tent and there was Elsie Charlton, setting up tables with the rest. You see, the real WI members stayed and got on with it in the end, no grudges. They made her life president of North Yorkshire and we were friends afterwards.' Not everyone was unhappy with the outcome. In Tyneside, one of the new Federations, a member said, 'As far as we're concerned, small is beautiful. We know everybody in this Federation.' On the other hand Northumberland, like many other counties, has to arrange county conferences in several different centres to ensure adequate access for its scattered membership.

'...greater involvement, greater enthusiasm, more brain-power feeding in fresh experience and contributing new ideas...'

One indisputable advantage of the increase in the number of Federations is that 'a far greater number of people are involved in running things. Five Federations instead of one means five executive committees with their attendant subcommittees,' says Anne Harris, referring to Yorkshire. 'Greater involvement, greater enthusiasm, more brain-power feeding in fresh experience and contributing new ideas.' The whole operation was an enormous upheaval, and even if a future government were to introduce new changes in administrative boundaries the WI may not necessarily follow suit. Enough, NFWI and members are inclined to think, is enough!

By 1981, membership numbers had become a serious preoccupation of Executive. As a result of rising subscriptions, some members left; age regularly removed others; the battle over boundary changes brought further losses. It was time to take a good look at the movement. Strathclyde University was commissioned to undertake a survey in depth of the WI as a whole. The report examined old counties, new counties, large WIs, small WIs, older and younger women, to see what they wanted from a voluntary organization. Non-members were asked too.

'...what they wanted first was friendship, then they wanted "to have some effect on things; they didn't just want to sit about"...'

The replies confirmed that what they wanted first was friendship, then they wanted 'to have some effect on things; they didn't just want to sit about', Anne Harris recollects. 'We felt we were doing all that. The trouble was, we were waiting for people to find us, not going out to tell them what we do.' It was time to set about promotion. A new project, Women in the Community, was launched and a committee appointed to plan a mammoth exhibition to put the WI more squarely on the map.

WI craft shows, markets, flower-arranging competitions had been staged at Olympia for many years past as part of someone else's pro-

motion; the Ideal Home Exhibition, the National Dairy Show. What about taking over Olympia entirely? What about making it the women's own show? Others could join in, but under the umbrella of the WI itself. Furthermore, it would be no modest light under a bushel but a blazing beacon. Launched at an AGM, the publicity machine whirred into action. National Express, loyal supporters as always, loaned a bus; the WI fitted it out with a mobile exhibition, and off it rolled on a countrywide tour boosting the WI image and setting the scene for the 'Life and Leisure' exhibition to come.

Launched from the steps of the Guildhall by the Lord Mayor of London, the promotion bus set off on a nine-month tour of England and Wales, with a succession of drivers – women wherever possible – and a great and changing rota of stewards. Meticulously routed and timetabled, it visited over 200 towns and cities, taken over by county executive and VCO stewards in each county to provide information, and by demonstrators to display their expertise in crafts or cookery. North Yorkshire tell the story.

'...the promotion bus set off on a nine-month tour of England and Wales...'

'On the 3rd, 4th and 5th of May the bus came to us. Before it came, we had to find suitable sites; where there would be plenty of people passing by, where it wouldn't cause an obstruction and where there

The 'Life and Leisure' exhibition involved every Federation and every sphere of activity.

'...they were just dancing in the aisles, it was wonderful. And of course, the press loved it...'

'...Olympia's "Life and Leisure" exhibition...'

was a power supply. We were able to park it for a day each in Skipton High Street, where it was plugged into a street lamp, Richmond Market Place and, finally, on a site outside the Prospect Hotel, Harrogate, where the Mayor and Mayoress were among the first visitors. We had arranged publicity, drawn up rotas of members to talk to the hundreds of people who visited it, and organized cookery demonstrations in the specially equipped kitchen on the lower deck. Upstairs was an exhibition of craftwork as well as displays showing every area of WI activity.

'The colourful vehicle was certainly an eye-catching sight and, as a result of its visit, new members joined and a number of places were pinpointed for possible new WIs. Two new ones, Jennyfield and Oatlands, were formed very soon afterwards.' The razzamatazz was uncharacteristic of the accepted WI image. At the AGM there was a parade of the decades, members marching up to the platform dressed up to represent resolutions that had been passed in each period.

'It looked good,' Anne Ballard recalls, 'and we had this jingle which had been specially written for us: it was very catchy. Some members didn't like it, they thought it was going to replace Jerusalem.' 'I looked down,' chairman Anne Harris says. 'Northumberland were sitting at the front and there was Betty Dodd. Everybody was singing this jingle. She looked up, winked at me, got up and started dancing, so of course, everybody did. They were just dancing in the aisles, it was wonderful.' And of course, the press loved it.

At lunchtime the chairman used to go out to talk to members. After all there were the vice-chairman and other Executive members who could look after the guests. 'I went out to the steps of the Albert Memorial where everybody was having a picnic, to have a walkabout. The press followed me out and said, "Go on, do some dancing here," then it started to rain. Someone put an umbrella in my hand and I laughed and said, "Look, we're dancing in the rain", so of course it made all the newspapers the next day.'

Preparations for Olympia's 'Life and Leisure' exhibition involved every Federation and every sphere of activity. Any promotion must be sufficiently wide to make every member feel herself a part of it. There was everything in Olympia: even the Queen, from Sandringham WI, was invited to attend. 'On entering the exhibition hall at Olympia, visitors were immediately stopped in their tracks by the sight of a huge mural of Denman College – said to be the size of a tennis court – on the wall at the opposite end to the entrance. The bus was there and a village hall had been built in the centre of the vast exhibition space, where VCOs were on hand to answer questions and give out information.

'Every aspect of WI life and activity was on display. Thousands of people thronged the hall to see the art exhibition, join in the sports, watch fashion shows and keep fit displays, buy WI publications, crafts or preserves or just rest weary feet at one of the many cookery demonstrations.' During the six-day exhibition, 55,000 people visited it, buying tens of thousands of craft items and 5,000 jars of preserves.

Olympia was a great publicity success story. The Queen enjoyed it; she stayed two hours, looking at and asking questions about everything, talking all the time of 'we' not as a 'Royal We' but as just another member. As Her Majesty walked into the hall a great fanfare of trumpets sounded from the gallery: 'spine-tingling stuff'.

The information stands were inundated with enquiries. Stewards took the name and address of every enquirer and wherever possible they were given the address of their nearest WI secretary. They were also advised to 'shop around, not every WI does everything. Look and find one which suits you and is handy to get to'.

'...shop around ...look and find a WI which suits you and is handy to get to...'

New WIs were formed all over the country. And the London group came into being. At the same time leadership passed to Agnes Salter, another Markets 'graduate' who had the knack of 'establishing instant rapport with a wide range of people'. As with Anne Harris, opening up opportunities for members was always to the forefront of her plans; new opportunities came about as a direct result of Life and Leisure.

Ann Macoun of the London staff co-ordinated the London group, with VCOs borrowed from the Home Counties. Four WIs were formed in 1984; Ealing, Chiswick, Fulham and district, and North-West London. Clapham, Roehampton and Kingswood-Dulwich were in the pipeline, with Richmond and Barnes to follow. Royal Eltham was also formed as part of the London Federation. A London-Welsh WI, incidentally, was already in existence in its own right: Llanfairpwll had come a long, long way. The standard of members was high, discussion at resolution meetings stimulating, VCOs reported back. These were people who were interested in life and in the countryside, prepared to be involved and who liked the self-governing nature of a WI.

'...a London Federation...'

At first it seemed right to form a London Federation. Initially it met in Eccleston Street, but soon the problems of travelling across the city at night overcame the advantages and each London WI joined its nearest Federation; Surrey, West Kent, Middlesex, Essex or Hertfordshire. This certainly brought them into the family; they became involved in the activities of Federations with both urban and rural communities, instead of looking inward to a city. In 1992 the London Federation was disbanded.

'...there's one thing, I know wherever we go I'll have friends ready-made. I can always find a WI...'

And a family is what WI is. When contemplating moving house one member said, 'There's one thing, I know wherever we go I'll have friends ready-made. I can always find a WI.' Some, like Cerith Ollerinshaw, only find it when they move. There are some lucky newcomers to an area who always get a 'Welcome parcel' from the local WI.

Travelling around the country, established WI members admit to checking local noticeboards to see what the WI is up to in any strange place. Cranleigh Afternoon WI in Surrey always have quite beautiful posters; a tradition started by Mrs Evershed who drew them uninterruptedly for over twenty years. Each was a work of art, 'well worth the detour'. Her successors feel the standard must be maintained.

'...each was a work of art, well worth the detour...'

As a further result of promotion there was a rapid increase in the requests for WI representatives to appear on radio and television. Press Officer at that time was Sally Diplock, who naturally played a vital part in all the promotional planning. Sally had come from the BBC, and through her contacts media training was initiated for the chairman, officers, general secretary Anne Ballard, chairmen of sub-committees and selected people from the counties. The consequence was well-prepared spokeswomen all over the country.

In the meantime, however, a new crisis loomed. At Denman College a relatively new Principal, Wendy Thorogood, had become unhappily aware that college safety and fire security systems left a great deal to be desired. New health and safety regulations made it clear that the college would be unable to pass any official inspection. Of course, if this came about, Denman would have to close. But the movement once again rose magnificently to the occasion, and the story of the 'Denman Million' is told elsewhere. Raising the Denman fund took two years, and in the meantime WI life went on; other leads arising from the Women in the Community promotion were being followed up.

'...the movement once again rose magnificently to the occasion...'

At Olympia a garden display featuring a special garden designed for easy maintenance had drawn crowds. Gardening is, after all, a national pastime, particularly close to the hearts of all countrywomen, especially Anne Harris and Agnes Salter. The WI demonstrated their concern for the countryside and the future of the railway network by launching a partnership with British Rail for Beautiful Britain, local WIs helping to cultivate local station gardens.

In addition, through *Home and Country*, a competition was launched to design a cottage garden. The winner would have her garden brought to life by Bridgemere Garden World of Nantwich in Cheshire, and entered at the 1988 Chelsea Flower Show. The WI Cottage Garden, designed by Jacquie Moon of Burton and Puddington WI, was a Chelsea show-stopper extraordinary, winning a Gold Medal and the Wilkinson Sword of Honour. Bridgemere created not only the garden itself but built the cottage to go with it: the countryside really did come to town. And to draw pleasure from a combination of cultivation and artistry, Denman invited flower arrangers to take over the college itself for a flower arranging festival, to thank all those who had come to its aid and to celebrate its new lease of life.

'...a Chelsea show-stopper extraordinary ... the countryside really did come to town...'

But the greatest surge of activity was in the field of sport, an activity not necessarily part of the standard image of WI life. While hunger, even starvation, are familiar enough in Third World countries, one of the ironies of life in the West is that plenty, not only in the way of food but of mechanized transport, home entertainment and a growing pleasure in watching others exercise themselves on our behalf, has brought with it problems of weight and even obesity. No surprise, then, that health promotion – including slimming – is high on the feminine agenda.

'...no surprise, then, that health promotion – including slimming – is high on the feminine agenda...'

At Olympia the stands promoting sporting activities had been besieged by enquirers; no one needed to be told that greater physical activity not only adds to physical well-being but improves the figure. Through a network of contacts inter-county competitions proliferated. The consequences were remarkable and in some cases spectacular. Bowls, swimming, tennis, skittles, croquet and darts were perhaps predictable; abseiling, hang-gliding, underwater exploring, ballooning, skiing and rock-climbing less so. One thing was clear: in keeping with the times and an ever-growing field of interests and opportunities, sport is now accepted as part of normal WI activity.

'...in keeping with the times ... sport is now accepted as part of normal WI activity...'

So, as the Eighties ended and the world entered upon the last decade of the present century, a movement which had had its origins in an unswerving determination to better women's health, education and opportunities in society could look with some degree of satisfaction upon its achievements. But in spite of great advances, the new social climate of the Nineties saw the return of enemies familiar enough to the older generations if not to their children now grown up.

Unemployment had come back with a vengeance, not only in the old industrial areas of Wales and the north but among the supposedly immune southern counties. Every region and every level of society felt the chill wind of economic change, if not immediately in terms of unemployment, then in a growing sense of insecurity that was no respecter of past patterns of society. Steelworks, shipyards and mines were the first to see the jobs go but it was not long before previously untouched fields of employment – white-collar businesses, hospitals, schools, banks – began to suffer steadily mounting casualties.

In the WIs' earlier days such things affected the women at second hand; a woman's place, by and large, had still been in the home with her children whether or no her menfolk were on the dole. Now times have altered: it is very often the men who are left at home while the women, full-time or, increasingly, part-time, go out to work. When working wives and daughters are the family breadwinners the change of rôle is accompanied by growing psychological problems, increasing family stress. Such developments impinge upon a women's voluntary movement such as the WI in more ways than one. How could the WI help both itself and others?

Educational opportunities previously available through local educational authorities have become increasingly expensive where they have survived at all. And circumstances vary from region to region. In Northumberland, to take one example, the writer was assured that 'we can get what classes we like since they're all subsidized because we're a depressed area'. A high price to pay, but things are not always easy elsewhere.

Classes considered as non-vocational charge higher fees than those leading directly to a qualification, yet may be equally helpful in leading an individual back into employment. The NFWI, fighting hard to achieve recognition of the work that its members put into the community, began strengthening its links with the National Extension College, the Royal Society of Arts and the City and Guilds Institute.

A new network of Voluntary Education Co-ordinators was set up in the Federations to liaise with local education authorities and keep open the doors to members' advancement. The job of National chairman is never a sinecure. Agnes Salter had an additional and tragic burden, simultaneously fighting a personal battle with cancer. She was supported to the full by the Executive and vice chairmen Jean Varnam and Wilma Mulliner (Dorset), but her last year in office brought her to the end of her life.

'...we can get what classes we like since they're all subsidized because we're a depressed area...'

Practice makes perfect. A student works on her calligraphy skills.

14: NEW TIMES, NEW MEASURES, NEW HOMES 1988–1991

JEAN Varnam of the Nottingham Federation was elected in 1988. There was no break in the flow of plans and events. The success of the WI garden at the Chelsea Flower Show augured well for the future as did the publication, in 1989, of *Village Voices*, a warmly reminiscent and delightful account of village life and WI history drawn from scrapbooks compiled by each WI.

In the meantime there was a seventy-fifth anniversary to celebrate in 1990. A single event, the NFWI decided, would not be sufficient; each and every WI should join in; the festivities would involve members personally. The Great Promotion of the previous five years had raised the profile of an organization adapting itself to the needs and wishes of new times and a changing membership. The momentum must be maintained.

'...the previous five years had raised the profile of an organization adapting itself to the needs and wishes of new times and a changing membership...'

But financial problems are always waiting to pop up, usually at an inconvenient moment, and this time they had a rather more personal slant. Here was a large and nationally respected body, shortly to be 75 years old, responsible for income and funds that had become dauntingly large, still run by volunteers. Costs in an inflationary age continued to soar; there was an endless struggle to keep the movement solvent. If income should fail to keep pace with expenditure the responsibility for any financial loss could fall, legally and directly, upon an unpaid, hardworking, wholly voluntary National Executive.

The risk was real; in a financial crisis – Denman burned down, for instance, before the 'Denman million' enabled it to meet the new fire regulations – the brunt would have to be born individually. The sums involved might result in Executive members' personal property, even their homes, being put in hazard. No individual member, it was felt, should be asked to accept that kind of risk any longer. The situation was pointed out by the NFWI legal and financial advisers. They advised the NFWI to turn itself into an incorporated company limited by guarantee. By this means any financial loss would be shared equally by the membership as a whole.

The lengthy process of bringing this about began in 1988. Many Federations, wisely understanding that new times require new measures, undertook the same changes. But as each Federation is also a registered charity, the charity commissioners must approve every step of the procedure and, like the mills of God, they grind slowly and small.

'...wisely understanding that new times require new measures...'

'...for "dear old Albert", the writing was on the wall...'

Even before the business began, the NFWI Executive were looking at various underlying implications. One particularly dramatic change would be the effect on the conduct of the Annual General Meeting. For 'dear old Albert', though it would take some time for the fact to emerge, the writing was already on the wall. On a lighter note the year began with a modest party for 'friends of the WI'. Held in January at Salters Hall in the City of London, it was the occasion for launching the Year of the 75th Anniversary.

Like her predecessors, Jean Varnam believed in 'listening and heeding' the members. She travelled 48,000 miles in one year, she says, doing just that, and in planning for the celebrations she bore in mind what the Strathclyde survey had shown; members liked national events in which they could participate, and conferences on topics which really concerned them. A Choir of the Year competition, sponsored by the National Westminster Bank, was already under way; so, too, was another, more active contest which would directly challenge individuals.

'...skilful – and therefore safe – driving is, or ought to be, a must...'

With Vauxhall Motors, NFWI arranged participation in a competition to find a 'Woman driver of the year'. Imaginative and challenging, it recognized a lifestyle which increasingly relies on the car. A growing number of young women spend many hours chauffeuring their children to school and back, going shopping, getting to and from work. Skilful – and therefore safe – driving is, or ought to be, a must.

The contest started in the Federations, with tests on driving economically. Just to enter and undergo the test was educational. Federation

The WI Woman Driver of the Year 1993 Competition. Susan Stockley, NFWI chairman, and Susan Seals, the winner from Derbyshire, with runners up Lorraine Irwin and Tracy Cobb.

Promoting a new image through the WI Woman Driver of the Year 1993 Competition.

winners went on to regional rounds, aiming for the final and the chance to win a new car. Federations set up day schools with the aid of the police and the Institute of Advanced Motorists. Families became involved and, as families do, became critical. Though less acrimonious than the average treasure hunt, it may not have enhanced the harmony of the home, but it did make for safer drivers, attract press interest and raise the profile of the WI.

But the first event actually to take place in the 1990 anniversary celebrations was the Calor Gas-WI 'Citizen of the '90's' competition, open to men as well as women. WIs were invited to nominate the person who had contributed most to the community and there were 500 nominations, 100 of whom were men. In an imaginative touch there was also a competition to design the trophy to be awarded, and the winning designer was by Shirley Peters of Carmarthen.

'...Calor Gas-WI "Citizen of the '90's"...'

The Princess of Wales presents a special trophy to the WI/Calor Citizen of the 90's – Fraser Pithie.

Simultaneously, things were happening in the regions. The WI has an impressive array of talents at its disposal: an opportunity to see them on display at a centre other than London was organized by National and sponsored by Nottinghamshire County Council. The Rufford Craft Centre in Nottingham opened its doors to many thousands of visitors during a month-long exhibition of WI arts and crafts. And the Welsh Federations were staging their own event. The National Folk Museum in St Fagans, Cardiff, regularly draws crowds to its beautiful setting. On this occasion a bilingual multimedia exhibition presented a video story of the WI, from that historic first meeting in Llanfairpwll

The prizewinning garden using the theme 'Our Green and Pleasant Land', at the Chelsea Flower Show, May 1990.

'...the principal speaker was Her Majesty the Queen...'

'...the future of one of the few remaining wildernesses became a matter of passionate concern...'

in 1915 to the 1990 anniversary. It ran from May to October, then headed north to The Museum of the North at Llanberis, where it remained for another six months.

The third event culminating in May had also required much forward planning. This was a second garden entry for the Chelsea Flower Show, the new theme depicting 'This Green and Pleasant Land'. The winner, Kate Chambers of Staffordshire, planned her garden on four different terrains. Bridgemere Gardens were once more the creators of the actual garden, and once again it was a gold medal winner at Chelsea.

A sad occasion for a great many WIs, the 1990 AGM was the last to be held at the Albert Hall. In that much loved if in many ways awkward building over a quarter of a million members had, at one time or another, experienced the thrill of being part of a warm and extraordinarily supportive nationwide sisterhood. The buzz as the hall slowly filled, the hush as the meeting was called to order, the spine-tingling outpouring of sound as 5,000 voices sang Jerusalem for what everyone knew would be the last time in 'dear old Albert' were to become part of the movement's collective memory. Appropriately for such a historic occasion, the principal speaker was Her Majesty the Queen.

Two resolutions of note were on the agenda. The first was domestic: that the meeting approve that the organization should become 'a charitable company limited by guarantee'. Then, in a planetary leap of concern, the meeting pledged itself to having Antarctica declared a wilderness park. The first resolution involved every village's reading a great deal of very small print. In a wholly democratic organization 'the top' may wish to change but the combined will is essential if the change is to be approved. To the credit of all those village WIs, read the fine print they did, and the motion was carried. Becoming a company had a direct impact upon their own future, but the WIs clearly saw Antarctica as part of their future too.

Discussed in every village and town group in the previous month, the future of one of the few remaining wildernesses became a matter of passionate concern. Could countrywomen do anything at all to influence events? They decided they could, and they did, and in due course Antarctica was saved from exploitation; well, at least for the next fifty years.

The night before the London AGM, the seven finalists in the Choir of the Year competition, from 200 original entrants, held their 'sing-off' concert in St John's, Smith Square, Westminster. The winners, Lyndhurst, Surrey, were happy to share their prize of £1,000 with their Federation, while second and third respectively were Glenford WI, and Gotherington, Woolstone and Oxenton WIs singing together. And there was another, high summer event to follow. In July the winning regional drivers for Vauxhall's Driver of the Year competition assembled at Donnington Park and rolled up their sleeves for the last and most testing trials. What a chance to show off! Not all of us think that we may be a Nigel Mansell manqué, but we know from the insurance companies that we are better safety bets than the men.

The judges were looking not only for handling and manoeuvering skills but a real understanding of how to drive in such a way as to squeeze out the maximum number of miles to the gallon. Putting their competence on the line were no less than 8,000 entrants, not only from WIs in England and Wales, but from their sister organizations in Scotland and Northern Ireland too. Now they had been reduced to 30. It would be nice to report another WI triumph but it was a Scottish Rural member who won a new Vauxhall Nova, with runners-up from Wales and Cornwall – a splendid clean sweep for the Celts.

But of course, no birthday is really a birthday without a tea-party, and the word had gone out early in the year. Every WI in the country would hold a tea-party on 11 September, the actual anniversary date. The parties could take any form, could involve the village or community at large, could be combined with a bring-and-buy or a raffle – anything that raised a little money – and all the profits would be put to a special and particularly apt use. The WI owed its own birth to the death of a single child: this would be a birthday present from the WI to children. Oh, and another thing; would all WIs arrange to have their village church bells rung to celebrate the occasion? Ask the village bell-ringers, of course, but if not, please make other arrangements because bells, everywhere, there positively must be.

'...no birthday is really a birthday without a tea-party...'

In Warningham, Cheshire, this request caused some little consternation: old age had retired the last of their ringers and the bell-tower was silent. But consternation had a short life in the WI. 'All right,' said Warningham WI, 'we'll have to ring them ourselves.' Seven members survived the long climb to the ringing-chamber and the first touch of 'bell-ringer's elbow'. Their tutor survived, too, and on 11 September the Warningham bells rang out with the rest 'in steeples far and near, a happy sound to hear'. Nor is that the end of the tale: the Warningham team stayed together, ringing for services and weddings, even bringing in new – and still predominantly female – recruits. They are now members of the South Cheshire Diocese Bell-ringers, intent upon ringing in the millenium and, in all probability, the millennial celebrations of the National Federation of Womens' Institutes in 2000 A.D.

'...the Warningham bells rang out with the rest "in steeples far and near, a happy sound to hear"...'

Nor were they alone in their determination to join in the general tintinnabulation. Tyn-y-Gongl and Benllech WIs lacked any church

Hethersett WI chose an Upstairs-Downstairs theme for their Edwardian tea party.

bells but, ever resourceful, formed a team of hand-bell ringers and produced their own birthday peal. And what a birthday it was! Tetley sponsored it to the tune both of the bells and goodness knows how many thousands of tea bags. They provided countless cuppas for every Institute in the National Federation, with Avon Federation mounting a Tetley Tea Run to deliver supplies to all their WIs and dressing up their drivers in carnival rig to do so.

'...tea for two? It was tea for thousands upon thousands...'

Guernsey had a Federation Mad Hatter's tea party with decorated floats. There were Upstairs-Downstairs tea parties, Edwardian tea-parties, Teddy Bears' picnics, parties for the old folk and the children, too, and, of course, more than one traditional tea-dance. Tea for two? It was tea for thousands upon thousands.

There was another notable party. It was held in the WI pavilion at the Royal Show as a way of thanking the movement's many friends and sponsors at that annual occasion. A few bottles of fizz, yes, but no caviare; instead there would later be substantial donations to childrens' charities from the monies the tea-parties produced. And the fund got off to a splendid start with a cheque for £10,000 from Tetley. Appropriately, the National Council met in Llandidno in October and enjoyed a reception at Plas Newydd in Anglesey as guests of the Marchioness of Anglesey, a former NFWI chairman.

Avon Federation on a 'Tetley Tea Run' delivering supplies to WIs prior to the day.

Yet, fun though they are, there's more to life than parties and competitions. Anniversaries are a good time for looking both forward and backwards, and for planning for the future after assessing the achievements of the past. The anniversary year was not yet over. In November 1990 the WI staged the biggest conference in its history, also throwing it open to all women's organizations. 'Women in the Nineties is the main event of our anniversary year,' said Jean Varnam. 'It not only expresses our opti-

The Princess of Wales receives a bouquet of flowers at the year-end celebration lunch.
Jean Varnam, National Chairman, on the right.

mism for women in the future but introduces a three-pronged plan of work for the next decade: women in the workplace, women in the community, and women in the world.'

'...women in the workplace, women in the community, and women in the world...'

We were already women in the community; through ACWW and our European membership of COFACE, as well as the way the WI nurtures its overseas contacts, we were also in and of the world. The position of women in the workplace was and continues to be under review. Conference speakers found themselves closely questioned in very lively discussion. Highlighted by speaker after speaker from industry, government and press was the changing rôle of women. 'Women who have entered the labour force continue to be the major domestic organizers of home and family.'

'Women have taken on a range of masculine responsibilities without shedding any of the feminine ones.' We recognize the age of 'the multi-faceted woman'. What is new is that such facts are acknowledged and talked about. In the national Press, MP Clare Short writes, 'Women do most of the world's work, earn little of its income, own less of its wealth, are absent from forums of power, do most of the caring for the weak, and suffer too frequently from abuse. All over the world, women's demands for an equal chance in life is the most revolutionary political force there is.'

'...the age of the multi-faceted woman...'

Quietly but firmly the WI and ACWW continue to gain presence at the forums and press their mandates home. And in the middle of a year which one would have thought would leave National Executive on its collective knees, headquarters moved from Eccleston Street to New King's Road. The staff under Anne Ballard coped splendidly.

'...quietly but firmly the WI and ACWW continue to gain presence at the forums and press their mandates home...'

Office move from Belgravia where it had been located since 1926 to Fulham, London SW6.

Questioned about it now, Jean Brewer, Anne's secretary at the time, actually had to think before answering, 'Busy? Yes, I suppose it must have been.'

In accepting the responsibilities of leadership a national chairman and executive committee sometimes need to take action in the interests of members without prior consultation. One such situation requiring urgent attention concerned the renewal of the leases of NFWI's London headquarters in Eccleston Street and Chester Square. In 1917 Lady Denman obtained the Eccleston Street premises at a peppercorm rent. The adjacent Chester Square property, acquired later, cost considerably more. In 1989 its rent was increased to £75,000 per annum, double the previous year, and would continue to rise, while the leases of both buildings had just over ten years to run. It was time to consider a move, and delay could be costly.

'...it was time to consider a move...'

A constantly recurring question in Council over the years was: Why stay in London when we're a country organization anyway? The answer was and continues to be that London is the most accessible place for members from every part of the country, and for representatives from government and other bodies whom we want to attend meetings from time to time. But to find new premises to rent in a suitable part of London could be prohibitively expensive, and to buy a new building outright appeared to be out of the question. The chairman, Jean Varnam, made a direct approach to the NFWI's landlord, the Duke of Westminster, to discuss the situation. She found the Duke more than eager to get back the leases on both of our buildings, which he could then sell on at very much higher rents to two separate tenants.

Mrs Varnam and general secretary Anne Ballard negotiated, 'long, hard and tough' with His Grace's agent. They agreed to sell him their

Display by the Herefordshire Federation.

unexpired leases for £1.3 million under his proviso that they should vacate the premises within nine months. This would give him ten-year leases to sell; if they went down to nine he would only pay half the sum.

Coincidentally, the NFWI's financial advisers raised some questions on investments: it was a good time to sell a particular holding of shares which were not performing well. This would provide a further £250,000 with which to buy a building which would be a fixed asset for the movement and simultaneously eliminate the need to pay an annual rent. The new offices had to be large enough to house the National Federation staff under one roof, to provide an office for WI Markets, for *Home and Country* editorial and sales staff, and be the headquarters of WI Books. It must also have good committee rooms and storage facilities, together with good communications. Ideally, what was needed was a good modern office block that would have little need for repairs or structural modification, and it had to be found within the time limit set by the Duke's conditions. 104 New King's Road fulfilled most conditions; near a tube station, on a bus route, modern and light, 'and it didn't cost members a penny'.

'...and it didn't cost members a penny...'

Moving away from the centre of London has had both advantages and disadvantages. The immediate gain is financial; expenses have been substantially reduced. Any building which is owned rather than leased becomes a financial asset. If it proves unsuitable as circumstances change, then there is something to sell. The rooms may be smaller and the ceilings lower than the spacious house in Eccleston Street, but that should make the space easier and cheaper to heat. Access by tube or bus is easy, parking less difficult. All in all, the pluses outweigh the minuses. So, subscriptions were raised to a more realistic level; expenditure was reduced by rationalization; earning capacity was increased.

With a smaller building and a membership that had shrunk more than a little over the years, the staff was gradually reduced. Some did not want to move; some retired. As for the NFWI Executive, a group of 'umbrella' committees took over the work of many small ones: everything was experimental and would have to prove itself.

At the concluding event of the year, a lunch for all the Federation chairmen and one representative from each of the sponsoring organizations, the highlight was the presentation to the Princess of Wales of four 'tea-party' cheques. There was a gasp as Jean Varnam announced the total; £100,000 each for four separate children's charities. This was the WI remembering the death of Adelaide Hoodless's child and the worldwide network of friendship and co-operation to which that sad loss gave rise.

'...the WI remembering the worldwide network of friendship and co-operation...'

Guernsey Federation's Mad Hatters

Anne Ballard, after twenty-one years' service to the NFWI, received bouquets both floral and verbal, but not every last thing in the movement's anniversary year centred on women. The Calor Gas-WI 'Citizen of the Year' award of £1,000 went to a man!

Anything following such a year was bound to seem somewhat anticlimactic. All the same, there was one unique event. The 76th anniversary Annual Meeting in 1991 was also the movement's first Triennial General Meeting. It was a legal requirement that the new limited company should hold regular meetings for representatives from every WI. The previous custom had been that one delegate could represent two WIs

Seventy-fifth Tea Party on the theme of nursery rhymes. Crabbs Cross and Hunt End WI, Redditch.

Now each must be individually represented. The most immediate problem lay in finding a venue large enough, central enough and with sufficient facilites to cope with almost 10,000 people.

Accessibility, in the form of good transport services, was obviously important. Space for every kind of conference facility – information services as well as seating for such a huge gathering – was essential. In addition there were such things as overnight accommodation, catering and entertainment.

Few places could fit the bill. In point of fact there was really only one. The National Exhibition Centre, in Birmingham, is about as far from the Albert Hall in style and function as it would be possible to find, but whatever one's feelings about it, it's hard to imagine what would have happened without it.

The Triennial meeting of the National Federation of Women's Institutes is almost certainly the biggest formal General Meeting to be held on a regular basis in this country; larger by far, for example, than any political party conference. And anyone who has been to the AGM of a major British company such as ICI or British Aerospace will know that attendance normally consists of a scatter of representatives of the Press and the major financial institutions, plus a bare handful of share-

'...the biggest formal General Meeting to be held on a regular basis in this country...'

Seventy-fifth Birthday Tea Party and celebrations, Crabbs Cross & Hunt End WI.

'...a night away from home and a chance to do the town...'

holders: even a WI Federation meeting is on a vastly larger scale than any of those business meetings.

To find anything remotely comparable with the Triennial one would have to think of open-air pop festivals at the Wembley Stadium. The Triennial may not generate the same amount of publicity, it certainly produces less noise but even so, nearly 10,000 women singing 'Jerusalem' ... ! Unfortunately there is a risk of its being marred by over-amplification of the accompaniment. One delegate to the 1994 Triennial turned to her neighbour, tears in her eyes, and muttered, 'They told me what a thrill it was to hear everyone sing and I was so looking forward to it, but I can't even hear myself!'

All the same, large-screen closed circuit television projection in 1994 managed to bridge the gap between platform and audience. And there is a collective willingness of delegates to listen, appreciate and, almost telepathically, project their response. In the old days, a trip to London for the AGM was a social as well as a business event, eagerly looked forward to by delegates as a night away from home and a chance to 'do the town'. It is not unkind to Birmingham to admit that what is on offer there is a different kind of experience, yet it says much for the membership that WI determination and standards of efficiency still succeed in turning the new-style Triennial into a memorable occasion.

And perhaps, by the time the third Triennial comes along, conference centre management will have solved the problem of what happens at the end of a meeting when 10,000 women who have been concentrating intently on the proceedings all want to go to the loo at the same time.

NFWI Seventy-fifth Birthday Tea Party and celebrations, Milverton & Nyuehead WIs, 1990.

15: TODAY'S WOMEN

ARE we still being realistic when talking about 'countrywomen'? What is our vision of rural life? Is it compatible with the realities of life in 1994? Villages of mixed households living amicably together, greeting each other by name, working in the vicinity of their homes and sending their children off to school in the morning on foot have largely vanished. The rural population has grown by an average 7% since 1981 and had done so by 10% during the previous decade. Yet agriculture occupied only 3% of the population over the whole. This varies considerably across the country; 30% in Shropshire and 29% in Dorset, and Northumberland still consider farming their main employment. Rural businesses tend to be small and employ few people. Self-employment accounts for 16%.

For the majority, now, a living is earned in the nearest town. And townspeople like to live in the country. 'All our villages are commuter villages now', say Yorkshire Federations. 'There are no tied cottages; they are gentrified and taken over by commuters.' Northumberland comment, 'They don't often join in village life, consider themselves too sophisticated. But few WI members wear straws in their hair'.

'...all our villages are commuter villages now ... there are no tied cottages...'

The decline of services forces rural communities to turn to the town. In a 1994 survey by Action with Communities in Rural England, in spite of an increase in population, 39% of parishes had no shop; 60% had no primary school; 74% had no GP; 36% had no post office. Local communities have to provide their own services as best they can. The work of keeping village halls active and in good repair is a considerable effort undertaken by volunteers, although some grants are available. Of the volunteer force active in the countryside the NFWI is by far the largest. In 1989 the Centre for Policy Studies estimated that the cost of replacing the voluntary sector would be more than £20 billion. 'When anything happens in a village 'they' expect the WI to do something about it. We're usually the last thing left in the place.' The WI are the people everyone turns to, keepers of the records; guardians of standards.

'...when anything happens in a village "they" expect the WI to do something about it. We're usually the last thing left in the place. The WI are the people everyone turns to, keepers of the records; guardians of standards...'

Women do not join the WI to provide a volunteer service; it happens that, as a focus for community life, requests for support in all kinds of things gravitate to the WI. In 1994 the most flourishing WIs tend to be in or near small towns or large villages, particularly where there are housing groups or estates. The older villages with static populations have the greatest problem in maintaining the WI and finding those still willing to take office. This is natural enough when, as ACRE notes, 'the rural population tends to be older. 8.1% of people in rural areas were aged over 75 in 1991, the highest proportion being in East Devon with 13.6%, and West Somerset with 12.7%'. As these are favourite retirement counties that should be no surprise either.

'...it's the 55-year-olds who give most. They retire early now and are still very active; no intention of sitting back...'

Yet in the Devon Federation they comment that their most active members are the 'early retired, they're full of go; lots of ideas'. Buckinghamshire make the same claim, 'It's the 55-year-olds who give most. They retire early now and are still very active; no intention of sitting back'.

Although WIs with an ageing membership inevitably close eventually, there is often a rebirth after a year or two. A new one will be formed in the same area by younger members, the phoenix factor at work. Many thrive and flourish with a mix of ages working happily together. Glenfield in Leicestershire and Rutland is such a one. Once owners of a good hall, they decided to sell it some years ago and invest the proceeds. They now rent the hall when they need it and use the rest of their income to nourish the WI. Every member has a free copy of *Home and Country*; they have several bursaries to Denman and support a host of lively activities. Just as Federations book Denman for a week so that their members travel together, Glenfield WI alone has been known to do the same thing

'...they enter everything, join in everything...'

Llanover in Gwent on the other hand is a small WI. Formed in 1925, it is still active and busy. 'They enter everything, join in everything', said their Federation. The village, little more than a hamlet, is charmingly picturesque and very rural. Its original president was the lady of the manor; its first treasurer, Annie David, a farmer's wife, was once secretary to J M Barrie. 'She treasured her WI membership', her family reported, 'she'd have had a dreary life without it. Her mother-in-law lived with them and she ran the farm.'

'...when the tree is eighty years old some loss of leaves, even twigs and branches, is inevitable...'

When the tree is eighty years old some loss of leaves, even twigs and branches, is inevitable. It would be a more serious cause for concern if no new growth appeared. 'Where there is already a flourishing WI we often have to open another', say VCOs. In Cranleigh, Surrey, there was an afternoon WI with a waiting list. 'Twenty-six years ago we formed an evening one with over 100 members. Now a morning one has formed and all three are thriving.'

Buckinghamshire tell the same story. They have formed several morning WIs. Two of these are for young mums; meetings fit in between taking kids to school and collecting them. At the other end of the age scale, morning meetings suit some older people better, too, 'to save

Caring for Rural Carers Conference, Church House, London, October 1994.

coming out at night'. On the drawing board is a plan for a 'lunchtime meeting to suit working members'.

Just as each WI is free to plan whatever programme suits them, so they make their own decisions about times of meetings. Abinger Common in Surrey always met in the evening; numbers were declining and meetings were not well attended. They looked at their membership and decided to change. No one was unable to come in the afternoon; even those who worked were part-time, so afternoon seemed better. The membership numbers jumped; it was a new lease of life.

'...membership numbers jumped; it was a new lease of life...'

'Mining villages are our growth area', said Rhiannon Bevan, then Federations of Wales Secretary, now NFWI General Secretary. She was talking about the Valleys, famous for coal and song. Now the coal has gone. In 1989 a new WI was formed in Treorchy in the Rhondda Valley. Instead of life centred around the pitheads the little towns of the Rhondda have become dormitory towns. Looking down on the terraced houses from the mountain tops, the streets are full of cars, 'not all insured and by no means new, but without cars how could people get to work?' The inhabitants have to travel to wherever work exists. Employment now is at Sony, the Royal Mint, Burberrys, in the new industrial centres such as Bridgend, once the market town of the Vale of Glamorgan.

'...mining villages are our growth area...'

Present day jobs now are not for brawn and muscle but for skilled fingers and delicacy. In other words, there are more jobs for women than for men. The WI has provided a new social centre and focus. 'The mining communities were very close knit. No one had to travel,

'...there are more jobs for women than for men...'

the valleys are very enclosed. The community has gone but the WI has brought people together.' When men were wage earners, were they the dominant partners? 'No, the women were always important; they cared and made the money stretch.' There's a good range of ages; some in their twenties, some over sixty, but the average age is between forty and fifty. 'We have no problem with speakers; plenty of good talkers in Wales.' 'We do yoga, handicrafts and tap-dancing and, of course, the choir.' President Pauline Worman works with the Citizens Advice Bureau so knows the problems of her area.

'...the community has gone but the WI has brought people together...'

South Yorkshire is another Federation where the WI are alert to the social problems in their midst. They face the effect on meetings of increased fear of violence. 'Women's lives should be a lot easier because of washers, freezers and all the labour-saving machinery but the status of women has dropped.' 'Respect for women has declined in proportion to their demand for equality in the work place.' 'Because of fear of going out at night WI meetings are not as well attended, particularly in the winter. Younger women with children face having to drive them everywhere as it's not safe for children alone.'

'...respect for women has declined in proportion to their demand for equality in the work place...'

The village of Elsecar has a very new WI, formed in 1994. This is another place which has seen social change. Once a feudal village revolving around its big house, then dependent on mining, its lord of the manor was replaced by a secretive company, and the pit has closed. The WI is certainly arriving 'where there is a need'. Elsecar has a new 'heritage centre' and there are efforts to create new jobs in the area but there were unemployed miners standing guard over the converted rail sheds, very willing to chat. They were going to classes 'to pass the time'. Is it time to start having some meetings especially for men?

'...is it time to start having some meetings especially for men?...'

Enrolling for the Women in the Nineties Conference at the Queen Elizabeth Hall, London, 1990.

16: WORKING FOR TOMORROW'S WORLD 1991–1994

NOT every year is an anniversary year, not every term of office demands something special in the way of ceremony and celebration. Susan Stockley of Somerset contemplated a period of calm and reflection to assess the situation of the movement at the beginning of the Nineties. The NFWI although still by far the largest women's organization in the country, had a declining membership. It was still largely run by volunteers in an age when voluntary workers are increasingly hard to come by. It and its small core of professional staff were faced, like many similar bodies, with soaring costs, falling income and a pressing need to decide its future course.

'...a period of calm and reflection...'

Over Eccleston Street years the breadth and scope of WI activity and the constant two-way flow of help and information between London and the regions had created a complex network of subcommittees. In the new premises, with less space to operate in, and a reduced staff to provide the services, amalgamation and rationalization seemed sensible. Yet creating a new familiarity, accustoming more people to operate on a national scale, is absolutely essential to the smooth and continuous transfer of responsibility from one regime to the next, from one treasurer to another, and to a progressively changing the NFWI Executive. National needs a very sensitive ear to the ground.

'...amalgamation and rationalization seemed sensible...'

Regions and Federations regularly produce their own events; information days, concerts, day schools, exhibitions, sharing their expertise and exchanging visits. This is where the action is: Cambridgeshire planting trees; Cornwall making an opera; Dorset exchanging with the Dutch members; Durham on the Orient Express; Gloucestershire having literary lunches; Herefordshire doing town walks; Hampshire studying nature conservancy; Jersey enjoying flower festivals; Kent spinning; Lincolnshire and Leicestershire baking and freezing; Nottingham house painting; Oxfordshire looking at St Helena; Suffolk planning celebrity concerts; Warwickshire forming a housing association; all regularly providing local focus and international contacts; Federations have scope for enterprise longer than the alphabet.

NFWI Executive members travel around the country noting, listening, discussing, bringing back their impressions to refuel the constant exchange of views at the heart of the movement. There is a wealth of experience and ability among the membership of the WI, although there are fewer people willing or able to make the commitment of time and energy which responsibility for any aspect of a voluntary organization entails.

'...there is a wealth of experience and ability among the membership of the WI...'

Above: Mrs Doreen Clarke, Kendal Castle WI, making a stone trough at Carter House Farm, Crooklands, Kendal.

Above right: Mrs Enio Gavclnev of Brigstear WI receives congratualtions from President Ms Stella Dicker on achieving an abseiling success. (Lakeland Echo)

Right: Cumbria Westmorland (Lakeland Echo)

Below: Gwent Federation WI walk 29 April 1987.

Below right: Guernsey members master kayak handling. (Guernsey Evening Press)

Above left: Having received a request for co-operation from a TV Programme, Isle of Man members turned out at Carn to exercise on the beach.

Above: Third Denman reunion, Lytham St Annes, Lancashire, September 1994.

Far left: WI cyclists with families near Stafford, September 1993 (first reunion of a Denman cycling course)

Left: Second Denman reunion. Canal at Aston Clinton, 13 June 1994.

Cumbria-Westmorland WI members stonewalling.

Kate Chambers, Hales WI, Staffordshire, designer of the winning Chelsea Garden in 1993, The Woodland Garden, built by Bridgemere.

While headquarters concentrated on keeping the wheels turning and the movement heading in the right direction, WIs and Federations were asked to put their collective wits to work to summarize the spirit and aim of the movement in a single sentence. A leading industrialist recently said that a Statement of Purpose should be an achievable aim for an organization, not the impossible dream of its chief executive. To decide what really is achievable, rather than 'nice if we could do it', everyone must have a say in what the aims should be. Certainly, the WI's single-sentence slogan – 'Today's women working for tomorrow's world' – is an expression of intent. It does not spell out the dream; it simply says what we are and what we do. Working for tomorrow's world means improving the present one in any way we can. 'Today's women' may be better off in every way than the majority of the countrywomen who founded their movement, but for a high and perhaps growing proportion of them, allowing for changing times, life is still relatively difficult.

The elderly – the over-seventies – often battle with shrinking incomes and a world that many of them find increasingly harsh and less understanding, particularly as longer life expectancy runs up against diminishing access to care. Those in their sixties should be enjoying retirement but may already be anxious about their future prospects as the cost of goods and services continue to rise and health services are 'rationalized'.

Actions speak louder than words. WI members fight litter with a will.

Between forty and sixty there is frequently worry about one's own and one's partner's job, in terms both of prospects and responsibilities. In addition, the prime-of-lifers all too often find their resources of care and understanding stretched to the limit in a tug-of-war between the demands of their children and the responsibility they feel towards their parents. Up to the forties life should, of course, be rosy, but here again insecurity of employment, not only for themselves but for their children as well, is already giving many 'thirty-somethings' more than one sleepless night.

Left: 'All in favour', voting at the AGM.
Above: Gold Medal WI/Bridgemere Woodland Garden, 1993.
Below: Susan Stockley, NFWI chairman, Denman Festival 1992, Focus on Europe.

So what's new? Some people will undoubtedly say: it's always been like that. And so it has, but what has changed is the rate of change and the degree of pressure. Things happen faster, sooner and, in terms of personal expectations and technological advance, with increasingly harsh impact in the event of failure.

And where does the WI come in all this? Well, 'today's women' need all their health and strength. They also need as much information as they can lay their hands on, and, above all, superior skills and as many qualifications as they can acquire. Officially recognized skills enable them not just to hold their own but to find gainful employment, whether in terms of financial reward or the satisfaction of doing their best for themselves, their families and their community. And in all of this they need support, encouragement, and the opportunity for shared, morale-boosting fun with their friends.

That is where the WI comes in, and it is in this general context that the NFWI must consider and implement its Statement of Purpose. Self-fulfilment, not just for personal benefit but as a contribution to the life

At the Examination Halls, Oxford,
for the first Livingstone Lecture.

Lady Anglesey opens Willow
Cottage, 1993

After the opening of Beech and Willow Cottages, the Livingstone lecture was given by Richard Smethurst, Provost, Worcester College, Oxford, pictured here with Lady Brunner.

Left: Elizabeth Southey, as Chairman of the Denman Committee, at the laying of the foundation stones.
Below: Lady Brunner opens Beech Cottage.

Cornwall's own opera, 'Little Women', staged in Truro. Beth attended by her sisters, l to r: Claire Libby, Emma Gane, Abigail Still and Carole Gill (on couch).

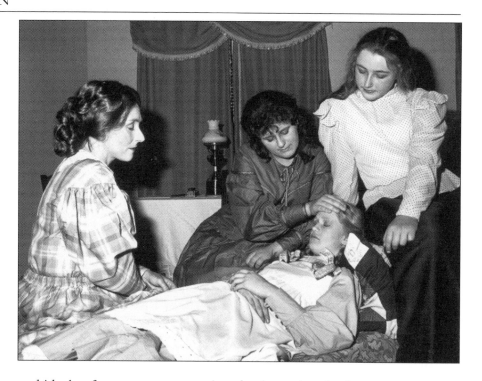

'...practical achievement rather than impossible dream...'

'...enjoying many a laugh in the process...'

'...their final weigh-in was a cause for celebration...'

and ideals of contemporary society, both rural and urban, to our country and to the world – practical achievement rather than impossible dream. In the matter of personal health and strength, regional sports co-ordinators throughout the country continued to organize and encourage sporting activities of every kind. Simultaneously, the NFWI and the Federations of Wales undertook a number of health promotion initiatives to raise the fitness of members and their families. Members joined enthusiastically in walking, jogging, orienteering, climbing, yoga and dancing, sampling a variety of sporting skills on an experimental basis with measurable benefit, and enjoying many a laugh in the process.

The Federations of Wales, since the establishment of their own staff and office, have a very close liaison with the Welsh Office, and pursue a number of issues on a national scale. In 1991 the entire membership set out to lose weight, seeing supportive mutual effort as more likely to produce results than solitary struggle. And lose weight they certainly did. Showing off with countless fitness projects, their final weigh-in was a cause for celebration: somewhere among those ancient mountains and valleys they had dropped seven surplus tons! Feeling that much the better for it, they followed up with a book of healthy eating recipes, *Simply Good Food*, published by WI Books, hoping to gain a few pounds of a rather different kind.

Health is not just a personal issue; the movement is involved in more formal ways. Susan Stockley represented the WI on the government's

Wider Health Working Group, which is considering how to create 'healthy alliances' to improve national health. NFWI Wales had already set an example of how to work successfully with government in matters of rural health, and the NFWI has been equally active, always with the needs of rural women firmly in mind.

'...equally active, always with the needs of rural women firmly in mind...'

In 1993 another project was launched in co-operation with the Royal Life Saving Society, to train people in the techniques of resuscitation and life support. The principle is to train teachers who in turn train others. The aim is to establish a nationwide network, so that in an emergency members of the general public would know what to do to save life. The network of contacts already built up across the country was sufficient to gain a gold medal in the Royal Anniversary Challenge marking the 40th anniversary of the Queen's accession to the throne.

'...a gold medal in the Royal Anniversary Challenge...'

So much for health and fitness. To forward the aim of providing members with information and the opportunity to acquire qualifications, NFWI drew up a policy action plan 'for the 21st Century' in 1992. In parallel with changes in national adult education, the NFWI plan gives high profile to learning opportunities in the WI.

Mavis Nicholson, guest speaker at the TGM, 1994.

A speaker from the floor at the TGM, at the NEC in Birmingham, 1994.

'...WI members take pride in their education ... We plan and learn together...'

In summary, planning and assessment is regionally based, classes and courses are organized in simple units of work in line with modern practice, and nationally recognized certificates are on offer for those wishing to take them. As always, learning opportunities aim for high quality and are based on good advice, and they will be used as a basis for recruitment of new members. 'WI members take pride in their education', the plan says, ending with a slogan: 'We plan and learn together'.

At the same time the 'travelling tutor' scheme was expanded, sending tutors out to tour Federations with courses planned at headquarters. In 1992, sixty-four courses were arranged, not only on such things as embroidery, knitting, singing and staging but also public speaking, committee skills and leadership training, Nor is training for regional tutors neglected. With the support of grants from the Department for Education, local education authorities and the Training and Enterprise Councils, the first part of the City and Guilds Further Education teaching certificate can now be taken within the WI.

All of which leads on nicely to Denman College, where operations were also expanding. Familiarity with Denman is an invaluable preparation for running the movement itself, and it is perhaps in the general area of education, be it health, personal betterment or the WI's rôle in national and international society, that Susan Stockley made the greatest impact during her chairmanship.

Judy Ward of Driffield WI, East Yorkshire Federation, at the Tockwith Multi-drive Activity Centre in May 1994, learning to drive a JCB.

The vital point about Denman is that it brings together every week members of all ages from every part of the country. They come to learn but not all learning takes place in a classroom. Having coffee, sharing tables at meals, taking part in the social life in general, they simultaneously share their own knowledge and experience. And as well as the Principal, the NFWI chairman or the chairman of the Denman Committee may also be there participating in the daily contact and exchange.

Opening new cottages at Denman College to increase student accommodation Lady Anglesey stressed the need to be 'flexible and ready for change'. Denman has over the years shown itself to be very adventurous and flexible and was more than just adventurous when it set out to contest the government's attempt to impose VAT on so-called leisure learning. The entire educational world was up in arms but the battle, said *The Guardian*, was 'spearheaded by the Women's Institutes' and a famous victory won through the sheer tenacity for which the WI is celebrated when it believes a cause to be just. In the words of a delighted Susan Stockley, 'They thought we'd give up, that we'd go away, but of course, we never do.'

Combining the change from European Community to European Union in 1992 with an excuse for an open-house event, the Denman Committee and staff staged 'Focus on Europe', a summer festival which brought a flood of visitors to enjoy the house, its grounds and the additional bonanza of a fair. So great was the rush – 3,500 members

'...the need to be flexible and ready for change...'

'...a famous victory won through the sheer tenacity for which the WI is celebrated when it believes a cause to be just...'

failed to get a ticket – that a repeat performance, 'Autumn at Denman', was staged in September and was once again a triumphant success. There were demonstrations galore, sports in the grounds, choral singing, recitations in the village church, handbells and bamboo pipes filled the house with music, and delicious food had everyone flocking into the marquees.

The summer festival was the occasion for emphasising the WI's European status. The many WI linguists made overseas guests feel at home, acting as interpreters and seizing the opportunity to tell them all about the unique Denman experience. 'Today's women' are only too eager for contacts with, and ideas from, the rest of our rapidly shrinking world. That fact was also emphasized at the highest level at ACWW's triennial conference at The Hague. The WI has always sent a delegation, but it is not always possible for the current chairman to get away to Australia or the United States, for example. Holland is no distance at all; Susan Stockley and her NFWI team joined with delegates from 63 other countries in considering ways to improve conditions for their sisters worldwide and 'meet the challenges of a changing world'.

In one of her monthly letters to members in *Home and Country*, Susan reminded them that one of the unwritten aims of the WI was to 'help leave the world a better place than each of us found it on arrival'. In another she quoted the ACWW motto: 'Think globally, act locally'. Both are part of the business of working for tomorrow's world and we can claim to have notched up quite a few successes over our first 80 years.

Today we have a standing and reputation of our own, particularly in anything concerning countrywomen and, indeed, women in general. The current vogue for 'networking' – getting your friends and contacts to use their friends and contacts on your behalf – has always been WI policy. The range of public opinion and interests we represent is countrywide and from all ages and classes. As such it guarantees that we shall always be listened to in the knowledge that any case we bring will have been carefully thought through, well-researched, and well-presented.

In 1993 the NFWI played hostess in the Palace of Westminster to members of the Lords and the Commons of all parties, strengthening existing contacts and making new ones. Whenever proposed legislation has a bearing upon subjects on which we are mandated to act – provision of adult education, the future of Antarctica, equality of age for the state pension, provocation as a factor in defence against domestic violence – we are careful to join forces with everyone whose aims are similar to ours, but we also take every opportunity to remind the legislators themselves of our existence and our point of view.

'...today's women are only too eager for contacts with, and ideas from, the rest of our rapidly shrinking world...'

'...the ACWW motto: "Think globally, act locally"...'

'...we take every opportunity to remind the legislators themselves of our existence and our point of view...'

This is the vital back-room aspect, less well known but in the long run more important than the WI's cliché image as jam makers. The calm persistence that gets rid of VAT on non-vocational education, the skills that win medals at the Chelsea Flower Show are both a kind of quiet power-dressing that makes the WI a force to be reckoned with in what is still largely a man's world. In 1992 we had another gold medal winner at the Chelsea show. This time the choice was a woodland garden, once again designed by Kate Chambers of Hales WI, Staffordshire, once again built by Bridgemere. It was even more of a crowd puller; seven royal visitors, a host of photographers. Three gold medals in a row has its spin-off in all kinds of unexpected but useful places, particularly when country matters are seldom absent from our agenda.

'...three gold medals in a row...'

And there was another national conference on country matters, jointly hosted by the NFWI and the NFU. Caring in the Countryside looked at the hardships faced by many rural dwellers. Closer examination shows the 'roses-round-the-door' picture of country life to be increasingly a myth, particularly as services, from transport to schools to village shops, are withdrawn. Isolation may be treasured by a few but, in the form of neglect, it is a real threat to many more.

Fewer buses and trains lead, of course, to more cars on the road, and Vauxhall once again sponsored a 'Woman driver of the year' contest. Again there were heats all over the country, jointly with the Scottish Rural Women and the Federation of WIs in Northern Ireland. This

Onward and upward; undaunted members reach for the skies on an abseiling and cliff-climbing course.

A tap-dancing class keeps in step. Teamwork comes naturally.

time we held our own, Derbyshire's Susan Seals taking first place and a brand new Astra Cesaro. As Derbyshire chairman Tricia Rees said, 'We were grinning all over our faces but she hardly smiled, just accepted it.'

'...one can imagine a kerb-to-kerb smile within!...'

One can imagine a kerb-to-kerb smile within! A major piece of WI community work was carried out in 1993. Following the implementation of government legislation on the transfer of care of long-term patients from hospitals to the community, the NFWI carried out its own study of the ways in which the shift of responsibility would actually work; how it would affect patients and families in rural areas where auxiliary services are often hard to find.

'...a survey questioned every one of the 8,600 WIs...'

A survey questioned every one of the 8,600 WIs in England, Wales, the Channel Islands and the Isle of Man. The resulting report, based on the responses of people actually affected by the new circumstances, was published in 1994 and widely publicized. A full conference in October 1994, with representatives from both houses of Parliament, the Carers National Association and Mencap, brought the circumstances of rural care even more firmly under public scrutiny.

This is becoming an established pattern of action; preliminary ground-work by the WI, discussion with all interested bodies, then a WI-organized conference to establish a public platform. The ability of the WI to undertake such activities, its expertise in doing so, and its networking skills in drawing in like-minded friends brings plaudits from government and society in general and, of course, requests for new help and involvement. And sure enough, NFWI were back at Westminster again in Adult Learners Week, this time co-hosting a reception with the National Institute of Adult Continuing Education. Lobbying outside Parliament to change the law on provocation in cases of domestic violence certainly attracts the headlines: careful pressure applied in the right place upon the right people at the right time is equally effective.

As the Minister of State for Education and Science said, 'we concluded that associations could help people play an active part in the life of their communities by promoting skills for active citizenship and ... informal learning opportunities as a preparation for progression into further or higher education or employment. I might mention here the

Waiting for the return of the adventurous climbers...'

'...careful pressure applied in the right place upon the right people at the right time is equally effective...'

leading rôle played by the National Federation of Women's Institutes in the development of community leadership training.' To name but a few!

All over the country in the early Nineties Federations were celebrating their own 75th anniversaries, some with thanksgiving services, many with concerts, theatrical entertainments, picnics on a grand scale and flower festivals. The newer Federations, too, were delighted to pass their first decade and some are coming up to a twentieth. But 1995 sees an even more significant event. Denman College itself celebrates the Golden Jubilee of its original conception with an extravaganza, Denman Fanfare. Colin Tarn, a great musical friend of the college, has written the story not only of Denman but also of Marcham Park, the former name of the house.

'...Denman College itself celebrates the Golden Jubilee of its original conception with an extravaganza, Denman Fanfare...'

In 1994 NFWI transferred to Denman the staff work involved in supporting four sub-committees, Home Economics, the Visual and Performing Arts, Sport and Leisure, and Training and Personal Development.

Susan Stockley, who completed her three years as National chairman at the second Triennial in 1994, was previously chairman of the Denman committee. Her successor, Elizabeth Southey of Surrey, has arrived at the head of our movement by the same forward-looking educational path.

'...the challenge of dramatic events...'

Some of our leaders have had to meet the challenge of dramatic events. Others have faced a long series of smaller but no less formative happenings. They progressed through countless committee meetings, annual Royal Shows, the opening of new accommodation at Denman and the college's summer and autumn exhibitions, the ACWW triennial at The Hague and a series of fact-finding exercises and conferences backed up by continual networking to make friends and influence people; rarely dramatic, endlessly demanding.

'...10,000 women whose one common factor was their belief in the WI and what it stands for ... our movement ... which gives more than it takes...'

Not everything in London had run smoothly in the aftermath of relocation, new committee structures and the consequences of turning the NFWI into a limited company. Yet life in the WI did more than just go on; it made advances. At the second Triennial, calm, cool and unruffled, the chairman, Susan Stockley, presided over a meeting of 10,000 women whose one totally predictable common factor was their belief in the WI and what it stands for. One felt admiration, not simply for the complete professionalism on the platform, but for our movement itself, which gives more than it takes, not least in training and encouraging those who begin as local WI members to advance, step by step, to become very extra-ordinary women.

17: LEARN AND GROW
Education in the WI

THE whole field of education in the WI is one of innovation, exploration, achievement and continuing progress. The process is evolutionary. Certainly women join 'to get to know other people', but they also come with a certain amount of baggage in the form of existing skills and talents, though they may be doubtful of their value. 'I didn't think I'd fit in,' one member says. 'My only skills were midwifery to sheep and singing in the bath. I found skills I had never tried before and some which previously I'd never considered of any value.' That's just what it's all about!

'...I found skills I had never tried before and some which previously I'd never considered of any value...'

The fields of knowledge on tap in the WI are wide indeed, and members start learning as soon as they join. To begin at the beginning, simply taking part in monthly meetings and, later perhaps, as a committee member breeds confidence. From then on, training in all the skills of running an organization is there for the asking. Public speaking classes build on first experience and add gloss. Personal skills are honed with practice: the shy and timid come out of their shells and speak up. Running things teaches organization and method; busy women do not have time to waste making mistakes or getting in a muddle, so they have worked out systems of management which are efficient and effective. The entire field of home and family is always at the forefront of WI activity: domestic economy, including running a home, feeding oneself and one's family, managing a budget, cleaning, decorating and furnishing. The skills involved in that faintly pejorative word 'housewife' are so many that when experts try to cost the work it is hardly surprising that they blanch and mutter in their beards.

'...the entire field of home and family is always at the forefront of WI activity...'

And though we may think we run a tight domestic ship, there is always someone, somewhere, who knows more about one particular thing than we do. Contrarywise, most of us have at least one little tip or wrinkle, or a particular depth of experience, that may come as news to our fellow members. That is why there are always classes in cookery, for example. Sometimes run for outside participants, more frequently they offer some imaginative or even exotic extension of the everyday. The same applies to other areas of household activities. Day schools are run in all aspects of renovation, home furnishing and decoration, with the the additional opportunity of gaining a recognized qualification.

'...they offer some imaginative or even exotic extension of the everyday...'

From the earliest days, knowledge of traditional crafts has been shared and exhibited. Exhibiting is as important as learning, because from

Left: In earlier times, individual WIs had their banners; this one is from Blechingley, in Surrey.

So many crafts depend on nimble fingers and co-operative effort.

display comes comment: could this be better done, and if so, how? Standards are set, achievements acknowledged, criteria established.

There are many ways of going about the business of self-improvement. The individual WI might invite a visiting teacher or demonstrator from the Federation. Alternatively, Action Packs can be borrowed from the NFWI. Devised by specialist craft advisers, these packs provide everything needed for a group to hold its own class. Starting with clear instructions and a list of the materials required, they take the student from beginnings to finished article, all without the actual presence of a tutor. This is an excellent way to learn as teaching costs and travelling expenses continue to rise.

'...Action Packs provide everything needed for a group to hold its own class...'

In 1994 there are seven categories of NFWI home economics certificate for those who wish to measure their own competence against a national standard. These can lead to becoming a judge and, or, demonstrator in a particular subject. In any given year the number of members taking certificate examinations is around 500, but this is only a fraction of those practising various skills. Close liaison with accredited bodies such as the Royal Society for the Arts has resulted in the gaining of qualifications which are recognized and accepted not only in the WI but also in the world at large. In 1968 the NFWI Design Award was instituted to single out those whose skills reached the very highest levels of talent, taste and artistry.

'...over the years the movement has organized many opportunities for work to be put on display...'

Over the years the movement has organized many opportunities for work to be put on display. In the early days exhibitions were open to almost all. Democratic and praiseworthy though this was, rejections caused heartbreak and hard feelings. Later events at Drapers' Hall in the City of London, the Imperial Institute, and the Horticultural Hall, Westminster, were for exhibitors who were prepared to accept much higher standards. One of the most exciting, 'Tomorrow's Heirlooms', held in 1975, makes clear in its name that today's WI sets its sights high, with the first, perhaps hesitant, steps leading all the way to work that will stand comparison with the very best of British craft achievements.

'...the combined effort produces work of great charm and ingenuity, as well as representing a very human record of the locality...'

In the Federations, crafts are a major activity; there are many local exhibitions and regular get-togethers for enthusiasts. Durham, for example, have 'Craft and Chat' mornings at the County House, and Kent have their Guild of Spinners. Many Federations have banners and wall hangings bringing together contributions from every WI within their boundaries. And 'every WI' means individual assistance from members who would not normally consider themselves expert craftswomen 'to WI standards'. All the same the combined effort produces work of great charm and ingenuity, as well as representing a very human record of the locality.

Examples of women's collective handiwork can be found in unexpected settings, such as the splendid patchwork stage curtains in Monkton Combe village hall, Avon. This project was initiated by the WI and largely made by them, but in fact involved anyone able and willing to ply a needle. Quite often a weekend visitor would find fabric, template and needle put gently but firmly into her hands with an invitation to stitch 'just while I'm getting the supper'. Then, of course, it was back to the WI to assemble the finished work.

Through the WI movement education for women in rural areas was hard fought for and hard won. It took time and persistence to persuade the powers that be that money spent on teachers 'out in the sticks' would not be wasted. At first, reluctant authorities subsidized teachers for limited periods, confident that their services would be underused and could therefore be withdrawn in due course. Not on your life! Classes grew and demand exceeded supply. A Board of Education White Paper in 1926 congratulated the WI on the teachers they had helped to train, recognizing the difficulties they had overcome in finding places in which to hold classes, commending the 'awareness that the WI have brought to village life' and concluding that the results 'can only be regarded as phenomenal'.

Things certainly haven't gone backwards since then. The battle for betterment was largely won between the wars. 'After 1944 a great burst of social activity in the country as a whole created a more sympathetic environment for educational initiatives.' In 1994 the WI continues to fight hard for the continuing right of adults to pursue non-vocational learning. The reduction of funding for adult education presents new problems and challenges for rural and urban students alike.

Above and below: Avon Federation of Women's Institutes. Wall hanging designed and produced by Avon WIs during 1992.
Below left: Clywd-Flint wall hanging

QUOTES FROM MEMBERS

WHY DO THEY STAY?

'They stay because they like the people; they want to fit in; they enjoy it; they think they will gain by staying.

'The resolutions feed my mind; the numerous eats sustain my body; the friendship lifts my spirits.' *Val Swarbrook, West Sussex.*

'The feeling that anything is possible; there are no barriers; the sky's the limit.' *Sheila Slaney, Staffordshire.*

'Friendship – doing things together and having fun. I always say when I leave this world whether to go up to heaven or down to hell, if there isn't a WI then I shall jolly well start one.' *Freda Houlcroft, Staffordshire.*

'Things snowball in the WI.' *Louise Lerpiniere, Kent East Kent.*

'I have gained friends, fun and a sense of belonging, never have to feel alone again. I can give as much or as little as I want in time etc. But no pressure is put on me at all. I feel really involved and very content with what I am achieving.' *Vivien Beckett, Middlesex.*

'There are opportunities if you want them. You can stretch yourself as far as you want to go.' *Karelyn Smithson, Suffolk East.*

'Family says it makes me a more positive person again, a quality I lost when I retired.' *Muriel Douglas, North Yorkshire East.*

'I have a WI family to turn to if the need arises. Helps me keep my feet on the ground, stops me taking myself too seriously and becoming too stuffy.' *Sheila Dooley, Lancashire.*

'I have trouble convincing them (my family) that membership doesn't automatically make me into an expert seamstress, decorator and chef; it takes a little time.' *G Savage.*

'When my husband read my report of my first council meeting he saw me in a new light. He definitely sees it as an opportunity to widen my horizons.' *Susan Rendal, Cumberland-Westmorland.*

'I didn't tell my colleagues at work that I'd joined in case it damaged my street cred. But when I told my husband he reacted with surprise and respect. "I hope you put that on your c.v. It's something to belong to the WI."' *Mandy Hoey, South Yorkshire.*

A high proportion of WI members never get beyond their village meeting, never go to a group meeting, let alone a Federation event.

Yet they still consider themselves good members; they help with teas; turn up to Bring and Buy Morning, do their share of knit-ins, make jhuggi jumpers, collect prescriptions for those without transport, keep the village hall garden tidy and probably go on outings. For them 'belonging' is enough.

Quotes continue on page 176

18: HOW THE WHEELS TURN

THE most important part of any structure is the basic unit; the individual WI; a group of women who have joined together, paid a subscription to fund their activities, elected a small committee to run their affairs efficiently, and a president to preside over their meetings. Elections are wholly democratic, by written nomination and secret ballot. Each WI belongs to a County or Island Federation (CF or IF); in most cases its area corresponds to local government boundaries. Each WI nominates candidates for service on the executive committee of this Federation, and votes for its selection.

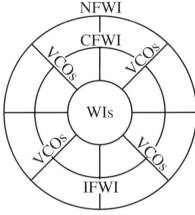

The WIs are at the hub of the wheel that makes up the organisation

The Federation executive committee chooses its chairman from among its members and appoints sub-committees to cater for the interests of WIs by arranging events dealing with its specialized areas of responsibility. Obvious examples are crafts, music, public affairs, international relations or even sport. However much the interests and concerns of members change, it is the responsibility of the Federation executive and its sub-committees to cater for them.

The NFWI Executive is also nominated and elected by WIs, although Federations likewise have a vote by virtue of their office. This is reasonable, as Federation officers have greater opportunity to meet and hear visiting members from other parts of the country, and are in a better position to judge their ability to represent the interests of the membership as a whole.

The NFWI is the link between Federations throughout England, Wales, the Channel Islands and the Isle of Man. The Executive committee of 'National' also chooses one of its number to be National chairman and therefore representative of the entire organization. One other group of women provides a strong bond of communication and continuity between the WIs, CFs, IFs and National: they are the Voluntary County Organizers, or VCOs.

'...a strong bond of communication and continuity...'

Today's Voluntary County Organizers are just that; voluntary, unpaid, and quite exceptionally hard-working. Members with a special talent for enthusing, guiding and helping people, they have been selected by their Federation to be trained by the NFWI to advise and assist existing WIs and bring new ones into being 'where the need for a women's organization exists'. The training, which is up-to-date and thorough, is partly on-the-job, partly at two-day courses around the country and finally at Denman.

'...voluntary, unpaid, and quite exceptionally hard-working...'

'...WI thoroughness in organization is self-evident and renowned...'

Training includes personal skills, organisation and management, public speaking, 'money literacy' and diplomatic expertise of a high order. Hardly surprising, then, that VCO training can be paralleled with management skills in the voluntary sector and industry. It can form part of an externally accredited award, the RSA Advanced Diploma in the Organisation of Community Groups, a nationally recognised qualification which the WI has been involved in piloting. WI thoroughness in organization is self-evident and renowned.

So the VCOs are the equivalent of an intermediate level in the general structure of management – a link between WI and National, responsible both to County Federation and National Federation. They are appointed by the NFWI after training, but annually reappointed on the recommendation of their Federation, which is dependent upon their continuing effectiveness within its boundaries. They are invaluable, and no WI can form or disband without their help, support and approval.

To ensure that the National Executive never lose touch with the views of the country as a whole, Federation chairmen and treasurers meet with the Executive twice a year 'in council'. Every spring, in London, the resolutions submitted for discussion at the General Meeting are chosen. At the autumn meeting, held at a different venue each year, subjects concerning the general health and welfare of the movement are discussed, and future plans considered.

'...the women who really make the wheels go round, smoothly, silkily and without fuss...'

No story of the WI would be complete or honest without talking about the women who really make the wheels go round, smoothly, silkily and without fuss. These are the General Secretary and the Federation secretaries. In London the post of General Secretary is vital to the health and strength of the movement as a whole. In Federations and at National these women are possibly vital to the sanity of their respective chairmen. Frances Farrer – Dame Frances as she became – was the hub on which the NFWI wheels turned for thirty years after she succeeded Inez Ferguson, who had served for ten – perhaps the most important ten years when all the basic rules and procedures were put in place.

On Dame Frances's retirement in 1959, Alison King took over and she too stayed ten years. It is no sinecure to adapt to changing chairmen and executives; they all have to be supported in different ways. Some of the general secretaries may have smiled wisely when watching *Yes Minister* on TV. They were not themselves as Machiavellian as Sir Humphrey but in many ways their job resembled that of a senior civil servant.

When Miss King retired, Meriel Withal moved to the front and held the fort for four years until the appointment in 1973 of the young

Anne Ballard. Anne remained with the NFWI until 1991 when the move from Eccleston Street was completed. She had served with and adapted to six different chairmen. Heather Mayall, her successor, had been an NFWI public affairs assistant before coming back to NFWI following a stint with another organization, and served for three years. All the counties, too, have their 'treasures'; many become very familiar, reassuring voices to WI presidents and secretaries seeking advice and information. It is to the county office that WIs turn first when problems or sticky situations arise. Executives come and go; some may continue to serve on sub-committees for ten or so years. Anne Ballard kept the show on the road for eighteen.

'...it is to the county office that WIs turn first when problems or sticky situations arise...'

The present, Welsh-speaking, general secretary, Rhiannon Bevan, was the mainstay of the Federations of Wales and the calm, still centre of the hive of activity which that office became. In 1994 it was Rhiannon who was persuaded to leave her beloved Wales for New Kings Road in London. Needless to say, she still keeps in close contact with Cardiff as she does with all the Federations. All branches of activity in the WI have benefited from the immense contribution of professional staff who have become well-known throughout the movement. It is only too easy to overlook some, but impossible not to mention Virginia Royds at public affairs; Vera Cox and Claire Balmer at markets; Anne Dyer and Valerie Duthoit at crafts; and Ann Macoun, now NFWI company secretary. Impossible to list them all. They all without fail respond to every call from Federations and WIs with courtesy, encouragement, ideas and solutions.

'...the immense contribution of professional staff...'

Now that a number of sub-committees have moved from London to Denman College as their base they will have more room and will be able to draw on the expertise and advice of the Denman staff. Erica Adams, who spent a number of years in London before becoming Deputy Principal, is a mine of information. Graham Jones is able to help on all matters pertaining to education, which is the basis of WI activity. They have all earned our great affection and gratitude.

Is this right? Expert hands add the finishing touches.

QUOTES FROM MEMBERS

WHAT HAS IT DONE FOR THEM?

"'I was afraid to go out of the house; I joined the WI and got involved with markets. I was in my own market, then county VCMO, then on National Markets. Now I don't mind going anywhere and meeting anybody.' *Mabel Purvis, Tyneside.*

In the WI one is always being asked to do something and you think, 'Oh well, if they think I can do it, perhaps I can.'

'I never thought of doing anything but I'd done some producing and was asked to do more, then take some day schools. I ended up as NFWI drama adviser and go all over the country taking public speaking classes. It's amazing.' *Rosie Bannister, Hertfordshire.*

'The more you put in, the more you get out. I've gained great friendship.' *Sandra Goldsmith, Dorset.*

'The WI is fantastic. I've made so many friends and found like minds and kindred spirits; had lots of opportunities to experience and learn new things; I particularly value meeting women of age groups I would not normally socialize with as well as other mums with small children.' *Melanie Gibbs, Avon.*

'I have built up a small business through the WI – a private functions room and I do outside catering as well.' *Rosalind Tucker, Bedfordshire.*

'I've gained confidence in dealing with people from all walks of life. I have learned to be myself and express my opinions honestly, have met hundreds of people and have received the same honesty from them. Whereas in my former employment I was 'appraised annually and thanked occasionally' in the WI people seem to take the time and trouble to show their appreciation spontaneously. The knock-on effect is my desire to be as helpful as possible.' *Dorothy Rawson, county secretary, Cumberland-Westmorland.*

'All the Fs – fun, friendship, further education, fizz, freedom, free speech, flexibility, fulfilment.' *Janet Foulsham, Hampshire.*"

Many more joined for the same reasons but once in, found an outlet for newly discovered talents and energy. Many found the WI a springboard to a richer life; gained confidence to accept responsibilities and win professional respect. Members as varied as Virginia Woolf, Laura Ashley and Gillian Shephard have spoken with affection of their membership. Others count the gains of a larger circle of acquaintance, friends, a heightened interest in the world and increased confidence as ample reward.

More Quotes on page 186

19: SHOP WINDOWS AND THE ARROW OF DESIRE
Public relations in the WI

THE general public tend to see WI members principally as craftswomen and cooks. Yet they are also crusaders in spirit, and aspire to better lives for themselves and their families; their resolutions are as broad in their implications as their field of concern is wide. The issues are not confined to the kitchen, though they may have been thought through at the sink, while driving a car, while using a typewriter or while standing in front of a class. Working for tomorrow is not only about creating a better world. It is also about nurturing a strong spirit. The encouragement of creativity, the practice of all the arts and a deepening understanding of the world around us are all part of the quest.

'...WI members are crusaders in spirit and aspire to better lives for themselves and their families...'

The arrival of the communications revolution has made it possible to do something about the WI's image. Through markets, local shows and exhibitions the WI makes its presence felt in its own neighbourhood, but nowadays many Federations make use of television and local radio to project the bigger story to a wider audience.

Television in particular offers a great opportunity for spreading the message. Lancashire Federation used a free 30-second community service slot to promote themselves, repeated at lunchtime, early evening and late evening in February 1993. It wasn't the result of a momentary whim; they had to apply for a slot, submit a proposal and wait for their moment in the spotlight to arrive, which it did at only a few days' notice. A WI willing to put on demonstrations at short notice was found, the Federation office had their script and display ready and everything went swimmingly. The broadcast brought in more than 600 queries, by letter and telephone, from women of all ages. And of course, it was not just potential members or even just women who were watching.

'...television in particular offers a great opportunity for spreading the message...'

Local radio, multiplying itself and capturing new audiences not just year by year but almost month by month, is equally if not more effective. Most women are not able to watch TV as they get on with the jobs, but the little transistor radio is the intimate friend of millions. East and West Kent, for example, shared a half-hour slot on Radio Medway in alternate months. Many counties compile talking newspapers for the blind; Kent-West Kent records *Home and Country* on tape.

Three Counties Radio is the channel for Hertfordshire, Bedfordshire and Buckinghamshire: one event eagerly followed over its seven-week run was a quiz competition among members. And a reputation for excellence can sometimes be pursued on a wider scale. Yorkshire Television turned to the WI for help when they wanted to stage Beckindale Show for an episode of *Emmerdale Farm*. And Constable Burton WI tracked down all their old wartime recipes to create a typical 1940s market stall for an instalment of *All Creatures Great and Small*.

'...no one makes lemon curd like my mother...'

The BBC tend to turn to the WI for authenticity in domestic matters, as they did to re-create wartime kitchens with WI's Ruth Mott for a TV series. And recently a comment from a TV presenter that 'no one makes lemon curd like my mother' produced a spirited response, Rachel Taylor cooking for the cameras in her own kitchen and turning up trumps with curds which were indeed 'as good as anybody's mother's'.

Of course, the public image is, to a large extent, what the movement itself projects, at Federation meetings and at National ones, wherever the WI appears en masse. And with women also invading the job market in large numbers, even though they are often only in part-time work, it is the older members who tend to have more time to be up front on public occasions. So many of the lively and energetic younger members, the ones who go on the sponsored cycle rides, make the occasional parachute drop, abseil down a cliff or test their car-driving skills, are normally at work and quite possibly bringing up families into the bargain; no time to help update the WI image when the national Press is around.

'...think radical. Think feminist. Now think WI...'

Things may be changing. A recent article in *The Guardian* began, 'Think radical. Think feminist. Now think WI.' Yet even in an up-beat piece on the WI's involvement with lobbying on the question of reforming the law in rape cases, the photograph chosen to accompany the article was of earnest women in hats, taken in 1965. National does its own bit to promote the WI. Apart from regular PR activity, WI Books is a successful public relations exercise in its own right. *Home and Country* too is both a professional publication and an ongoing PR operation. If the media want to know more about the WI they could do worse than read its magazine, and its newsletters, where the activities of members are reported all the time.

With such a spread of WIs across the miles of rural Britain, each Federation has its own news sheet. Some are simple, some quite elaborate, with contributions coming in from correspondents in every village, and of course the grapevine is a wonderfully efficient plant. But the chief organ of communication is *Home and Country*. Lively and well-produced, it is both the national magazine and another WI shop window.

Promoting the WI at the Flower Show in the grounds of Wilton House, 1980s.

With a current circulation of 85,000 and an estimated readership of around 350,000, including the husbands and families of members, it is the least expensive of all women's magazines, yet its articles and features have a very varied spread: financial management, food and wine, the Archers and a celebrity profile compete for space with book reviews and cycling the Pilgrim Way to Santiago de Compostela. In addition there is fashion and, of course, excellent cookery features. The only thing it does not go in for is sex, at any rate as a 'how to do it' activity. That, as well as its modest price, certainly makes it 'different' among women's magazines but it does nevertheless look at sexual issues knowledgeably, AIDS and premenstrual stress for instance.

New writing talents are encouraged, and contributions come from members as well as outside commissions. There's up-to-date news on Federation, National and international activities. The recent editor, Penny Kitchen, maintained a high profile in the movement, regularly going out to mix with her readers at Federation meetings and liaising with representatives in each Federation who are trained to give pep talks about the magazine in their respective regions.

'...new writing talents are encouraged, and contributions come from members as well as outside commissions...'

The small ads are also worth a mention: no need to look far if you fancy a B and B break in a guest house or cottage. The fact that it more than likely belongs to a fellow member is virtually a guarantee of quality and value. Today's women are in the market for today's world; Suffolk to Spain, Cumberland to the Canaries.

But back, if you like, to jam. Even in this basic area of public relations, the standards set are formidable, and they all come together in the most public PR exercise of all. The NFWI forms an integral part of the Royal Agricultural Society's annual celebration of rural life. Every year a different designer and team combine to mount an exhibition of WI activities in a variety of fields, as well as providing a press and information stand, a place where WI Markets can operate, and a stall for WI Books and *Home and Country*. The central exhibit is always designed to be eye-catching, attractive to the general public and in consequence a shop-window for the organisation. In the 1994 Royal Show the theme in the WI pavilion was 'Carnival'. The colour scheme throughout the display was red and gold, from the ribbons on the stewards' hats to the information leaflet any visitor could have for the asking.

Although until 1994 the WI had a presence at this most prestigious of agricultural celebrations, it was not always in a permanent pavilion. When show stands were allocated to exhibitors on an annual basis the WI could never be sure that they would have the space they had occupied the previous year, nor whereabouts in the showground it would be situated.

One year the team arrived at the Royal Show to set up their exhibit and discovered that they had a sloping site to contend with. Just as if they were having to steady a wobbly table in a restaurant, they tried adjustment after adjustment of their own tables with whatever underpinning they could lay their hands on but became increasingly exasperated at their failure to achieve level surfaces for their displays. Success, when it finally came, was only after a great deal of trial and error. Joan Lash, former NFWI vice chairman and a humourous as well as formidable personality, marched into the next Executive meeting bearing a large golden arrow. Painted down one side was a series of measurements. 'That's the difference between one side of the tent and the other,' she said, indicating two marks. 'That's what we have to contend with, and that,' thumping the arrow on the table, 'is my arrow of desire. I want a level floor!'

The WI presence was a strong attraction at the show; other exhibitors were delighted to be our neighbours, since we brought in the crowds. The heartfelt cry went out to the Royal Agricultural Society: why couldn't the WI have a permanent site? On level ground, so that they could plan their display in advance? The cry was heard and the WI acquired a site and a pavilion.

'...the Royal Agricultural Society's annual celebration of rural life...'

'...the theme in the WI pavilion was Carnival...'

'...that is my arrow of desire. I want a level floor!...'

Above: A dragon cake from North Yorkshire East.
Top left: The WI pavilion at the Royal Show with the Royal Show steel band.

Left: Carnival masks on display at the Royal Show, each from a different county, 1994.
Below left: All calm backstage – Leicestershire and Rutland catering for the Royal Show.
Below right: WI customers out front.

All Federations are involved in 'the Royal' through annual inter-county competitions. For the 'Carnival' theme in 1994 the designer was Sylvia Bolt of West Sussex, helped by Monica Saulle of Essex. Each Federation designed and submitted a carnival mask, a fabric clown of specified size, and a cake for children, iced to a theme. Against a background of these fantastic and exquisitely made carnival masks was a carousel on which clowns in dazzling variety rode their horses above a circle of cakes so stunningly conceived and iced that it would have been little short of sacrilege to cut them.

'...fantastic and exquisitely made carnival masks...'

In addition to these set-pieces there were demonstrations on how to paint canal narrowboat artefacts, cook for parties, make toys and practise a variety of quick and easy crafts. Outside the pavilion, regional sports co-ordinators organized fairground games, with prizes for the venturesome. Although the advertising of skills in a shop window is the basic purpose of all such shows, they also give the Federations an opportunity to display their talents to advantage. There is consequently always a queue of Federations awaiting the chance to cater at the Royal.

'...an opportunity to display their talents to advantage...'

It is no sinecure: the organization required to feed about 12,000 people over a hectic four days is formidable for non-professionals who nevertheless take pride in offering a professional service. The truth is that they are professionals, their skills honed to a sharp edge by years of similar if smaller events. Leicestershire and Rutland Federation, caterers from 1992 to 1994, developed their services to the very highest level.

Discussing the daunting logistics, Federation chairman Barbara Gill was very matter-of-fact. 'After we've made £10,000 it's all profit. Labour is free and there's no shortage of that.' A stream of customers passes through the marquee from morn till evening. All are dealt with and never a visible hitch: babies' bottles and farmers' flasks filled, even potential rivals handled with efficiency and good humour.

'...babies' bottles and farmers' flasks...'

At the 1994 Royal Show the WI marquee had Marks & Spencer as its neighbour, not only displaying M&S food products but actually selling sandwiches. The fact that a few M&S customers subsequently occupied WI chairs and tables while they ate their sandwiches may have caused a little behind-the-scenes irritation but the compensation came in the form of M&S staff, who came to buy their breakfast from the WI.

In return for such Herculean effort her Federation, from their hard-earned profit, will see their county office completely computerized with a bit left over for the kitty, while the WI's image benefits from public respect for high skills, quality, competence and unfailingly friendly service. The pursuit of excellence? WIs throughout the land have been chasing that particular quarry for the last eighty years.

'...the pursuit of excellence...'

20: TOWARDS THE MILLENIUM

WE are looking at a well-structured and very well-run organization, designed to serve the interests of women, with a well-deserved reputation for competence and sound judgement which has been hard-earned over many years. What is less known or recognized is the adaptability, the talent for innovation and the willingness to explore new fields which have characterized its history.

The membership in 1994 was just below 300,000, less than in its peak years but hardly an insignificant figure. Nevertheless, membership figures are a barometer of a healthy organization. Members leave through natural wastage; what is important is whether new members are joining or new WIs being formed. Each Federation reports new formations. That they are rather different from many of the older ones is evident in the timing of their meetings as much as their membership. Many are being held in the mornings, some in areas which are 'not healthy places to be at night'.

VCOs have ideas on the future. 'The core membership is strong', reports Huntingdon and Peterborough's Tracy Sortwell. 'We suffer from our own success. We show them what they can do, then they go away and get jobs and have less time to run the WI.' Then what about Tracy herself who is obviously from the same professionally-active age group? 'Oh yes, I've got a job which I couldn't have done without all the experience I've gained from the WI. I do market research and I wouldn't have had the confidence to talk to complete strangers, as I have to do, without WI training.' Does this mean she gives less time to WI? Not a bit. As VCO, county vice chairman and National steward she seems as heavily committed as ever and obviously loves it.

In Devon, Pat Macdonald feels, 'This wonderful organization has done so much for so many people, it should be better recognized. There is something for everyone. It has so much to offer. It isn't always clear at ordinary WI level just what is available through membership.' It is acknowledged everywhere that the president and secretary can make or break a WI. Everything depends on their enthusiasm, their ability and willingness to keep meetings friendly, interesting and stimulating. There needs to be some turnover of office. Everyone runs out of ideas sooner or later and it is good to have fresh faces to look at, fresh voices to listen to. In Devon they 'nourish the roots. We have talk shops where all new committees are invited and we throw ideas around, get everyone involved'.

The author, Gwen Garner

'...the core membership is strong...'

'...this wonderful organization has done so much for so many people, it should be better recognized. There is something for everyone. It has so much to offer...'

In Buckinghamshire, Stephanie Whitehead is enthusiastic about support for groups. 'The group system is important for getting presidents together. We have a VCO as liaison with every group, meeting them regularly and giving them a focus.'

Liz Mitchell in South Yorkshire believes in talent spotting. 'When you get someone fresh, with lots of ideas, they should be encouraged.' An older member recalls, 'When I was first on committee they wanted a money raising effort. I suggested a fashion show. "Oh, we can't do that," rose a chorus. The president put up a hand, "Don't ever curb enthusiasm," she said, and to me, "Carry on. What do we have to do?" We did have a show and the whole village got involved and loved it.'

'...don't ever curb enthusiasm...'

There is a general consensus that the roots must be stimulated, fertilized and supported. 'No good always expecting them to come to county things, you have to go to them.'

The good WI acts as a catalyst for social cohesion in a community. 'It should radiate warmth to all sections of the village.' They have to ensure that 'it's the place to be'. It should involve and entertain.

'The WI is going in the right direction, our eyes are open to the wider issues; we're not too parochial. Yet it's important that some of the more timid shouldn't feel pressured or intimidated by the power-woman image. There's a place for the safe, little WI,' thinks Jacquie Wylie of Northumberland. A good WI can be small or large. 'There's one I went to recently. They have nine members so all of them are the committee, do everything together. They enter everything, are happy and very go-ahead.'

'...a good WI can be small or large...'

Is there a typical WI member? 'There's a special mature kind of person who joins and takes a choice of what's on offer. It's nothing to do with age, some of our older members have a very young outlook.' Is there cause for concern about membership? 'We shouldn't panic. I feel there's a time when women are ready for the WI. It doesn't necessarily fit in with some younger women's life style. We may be trying to recruit too soon, targeting before they're ready, before they're mature enough.' 'You can join on whatever level you like, just enjoy your own group or go on, become involved in anything. It allows for expansion.' Younger members may only want 'darts and fun', as Sheila Tock of Durham comments, 'but everything else is there when they're ready'.

'...is there a typical WI member?...'

How about the future of the whole movement? Jean Varnam mentions collaboration with other women's organizations. Perhaps by joining forces? 'Our aims are the same as Townswomen's Guilds. We have no difficulties over that. There's a case to be made for sharing resources. I

Two VCOs looking to the future: Northumberland's Jacquie Wylie (far left) and Huntingdon and Peterborough's Tracy Sortwell (left).

wouldn't rule it out.' 'In an ideal world we might combine,' says Susan Stockley. 'Certainly we could work very well together on a national level but the members of both organizations want to keep their identities clear. We each have our separate foundations and traditions. It's important to preserve individuality, while acknowledging all we have in common.'

'...it's important to preserve individuality, while acknowledging all we have in common...'

NFWI can maintain contact with its most remote parts because each NFWI member is in close touch with her roots. Big events are wonderful for stimulating ideas and an inspiration to do something new, but London is a long way away for ordinary members. Regional exhibitions such as the Northern Arts Festival at Beamish College promote inter-regional, inter-county co-operation and show a different public what the WI is and does. 'Yet there is nothing to compare with the pride of an individual or a small WI gaining national recognition,' says Susan. 'I can't tell you how wonderful it was to get to London and sing with our small Somerset choir in a national competition. And it does promote the WI.'

NFWI needs to foster relations with all the Federations. They are now doing that. Each member of the Executive has a special responsibility for a particular region. 'We must avoid insularity.' The strength of WI is the friendship and support that women give one another. 'You plug into a power supply when you join. You don't realise it straight away, but if you need it, it's there.' And that power supply, the WI spirit, is immortal.

'...you plug into a power supply when you join ... the WI spirit is immortal...'

QUOTES FROM MEMBERS

**CONFIDENCE IS A
RECURRING THEME.**

"'I was extremely shy. I'd blush scarlet if picked out in public, now I'm secretary and can get up and speak quite happily.' *Pat How, Huntingdonshire and Peterborough.*

'On the experience of running one WI and through the committee became President of the Women's Society of my professional institute and ... the first woman in 120 years to be President of the Institute of Chartered Accountants. I needed that initial experience, that boost to my confidence ... I enjoy the chance to return ... each month to friendly faces who are just as interested in the other aspects of my life.' *Joan Bingley, Cobham Evening WI, Surrey.*

'I couldn't do that! That was the kind of person I was but now I could have a go at anything. This attitude took me to teacher training college at the age of 38. Result, qualification and eventual headship. I love it! And I teach tap dancing to WI members, that had been my other choice of career. So I've got it made, haven't I?' *Muriel Rutherford, Buckinghamshire.*

'An OBE for services to agriculture ... currently Master of the Worshipful Company of Farmers – the first lady they ever had ... Trustee ... of the Royal Show ... so the WI has a lot to answer for.' *Ann Wheatley-Hibbard, Wiltshire.*

'My family say I have come out of my shell. My confidence has grown so much I sat four 'A' levels and got good grades – in my sixtieth year. I have enjoyed classes in creative writing, communicating with the deaf, and three-dimensional découpage. It has given me the will to work and the incentive to succeed.' *Audrey Bean, South Cave, East Yorkshire.*

'Greatest gain – is in self-confidence. Knowing you can speak in public, organize an event, hold down a job in your own WI or at county level.' *Mary Jackson, Little and Great Oakley WI, Northamptonshire.*

'The Federation put my name forward for the Social Security Appeals Tribunal. I also represented the WI ... on the Executive of the Wiltshire Community Council ... Rural Initiatives Fund, Village Ventures and Country Pump. My name was forwarded for consideration as a magistrate and I was appointed ... all through contacts made through the WI.'"

APPENDIX I

IMPORTANT EVENTS IN WI HISTORY

1897 February 19: First Women's Institute formed at Stoney Creek, Ontario, Canada

1915 September 11: First Women's Institute in England and Wales formed Llanfair PG., Anglesey, Wales

1917 September: First County Federation formed – Sussex
October: First Annual General Meeting (AGM) of WI delegates
National Federation of Women's Institutes (NFWI) formed
Lady Denman first Chairman

1918 First National Handicraft Exhibition
Voluntary County Organizers appointed and first VCO training school

1919 March: First number of *Home and Country* published
Consultative Council set up
General Endowment Fund started
The NFWI becomes self governing

1920 Guild of Learners of Handicrafts formed (Handicrafts Guild)

1922 Handicrafts Exhibition at Victoria and Albert Museum

1923 Formation of Welsh Counties Conference
AGM decides that WI membership is open to women and girls only

1926 NFWI's claim for exemption from Income Tax allowed on appeal
Board of Education White Paper commends WIs

1927 Financial independence of NFWI

1929 National Council of Social Services request NFWI to help unemployed

1932 AGM decides that the fares of all the delegates to the meeting should be pooled
Resolution to organize and increase WI Co-operative markets.

1933 Associated Country Women of the World (ACWW) started

1934 NFWI delegate to International Peace Conference in Geneva

1937 WI celebrates twenty first birthday

1939 Produce Guild formed
WIs help in evacuation scheme
First grant from Development Commission for agricultural work

1940 First grant from Ministry of Food; NFWI begins to administer Ministry of Food's fruit preservation scheme

1943 Only wartime AGM decides to adopt linking system because of size of organisation

1945 AGM instructs NFWI Executive Committee to establish a WI College

1946 First Combined Arts Festival
CUKT grant to start WIs in Channel Islands

1948 Denman College opened
First grant received from the Ministry of Education 'for the development of liberal education for women'.
Home Produce Exhibition
Second Report on Constitution

1949 First WI in the Isle of Man formed

1950 'Folk Songs of the Four Seasons' by Ralph Vaughan Williams performed at the Albert Hall by WI choirs

1951 First Market Place at Ideal Home Exhibition, Olympia

1952 Crafts Exhibition at Victoria and Albert Museum
Malayan Government invites WI to start Malayan WIs

1955 Keep Britain Tidy Group formed, following WI resolution

1957 Drama Festival 'Out of this Wood'

1958 Market Place at Ideal Home Exhibition, Olympia

1959 WI contributes to World Refugee Year

1961 Resolution pledging WIs to support the Freedom from Hunger campaign

1962 Country Feasts and Festivals Competition at Dairy Show

1963 First National Art Exhibition, 'Painting for Pleasure', at the Galleries of the Federation of British Artists
First WI in psychiatric hospital

1965 Golden Jubilee year – 'Golden Market Place' Ideal Home Exhibition, Olympia. Rule limiting formation of WIs to places with under 4000 population rescinded
WI 'Scrapbooks of the Countryside'

1966 WI Freedom from Hunger Fund closed
National Appeal for half a million pounds launched

1969 'The Brilliant and the Dark' performed in the Royal Albert Hall
Aim of national Appeal (over £500,000) realised

1970 New teaching centre opened at Denman College by HM The Queen Mother
Third report on the constitution
WI involvement in European Conservation year

1971 AGM resolution changes interpretation of the non-party political and non-sectarian rules
WI member Mrs O Farquharson elected World President of ACWW

1972 'This Green and Pleasant Land' exhibition at Olympia
Produce and Handicrafts Guilds ceased

1975 Diamond Jubilee
WI involvement in European Architectural Heritage Year
'Tomorrow's Heirlooms' Exhibition

1976 Approval of new methods of charging subscription

1977 Registration of WI Books Ltd
'Jam and Jerusalem', a history of the WI, published

1979 Home Economics centre at Denman College opened by
HM the Queen

1980 National Festival of Creative Entertainment, 'Scene 80', performed at Stratford on Avon

1981 National Council replaces Consultative Council

1982 Three public performances of 'Early One Morning'

1983 '*WI – Women in the Community*' promotion launched

1984 'Life and Leisure' exhibition at Olympia

1985 70th Anniversary
£1 million appeal launched for Denman College
WI Festival of Sport at Bath University

1987 Flower Festival at Denman College

1988 WI/Bridgemere win Gold Medal and Wilkinson Sword Award
for the Country-woman's Garden at Chelsea Flower Show

1989 Home and Country celebrates 70th anniversary and publishes a
nostalgic book of extracts from the magazine

1990 75th Anniversary
AGM addressed by HM the Queen
'Women in the Nineties' conference sponsored by Marks & Spencer
Vauxhall WI Woman Driver of the Year competition
WI Calor Gas 'Citizen of the 90s'
WI/Bridgemere Chelsea Gold Medal for the garden 'This
Green and Pleasant Land'
NFWI becomes a charitable company limited by guarantee
WI National Art Exhibition Rufford, Nottinghamshire
WI National Westminster Choir Festival St Johns, Smith
Square, London
NFWI headquarters move from Belgravia to Fulham
Federations of Wales exhibition at the Welsh Folk Museum,
St Fagans, Cardiff

1991 First Triennial General Meeting (TGM) at the National
Exhibition Centre, Birmingham

1992 'Focus on Europe' and 'Autumn at Denman'
Festivals at Denman
NFWI/RLSS Life Support project wins gold award in Royal
Anniversary Challenge to celebrate HM the Queen's
40th anniversary

1993 First WI House of Commons reception
Inaugural Sir Richard Livingstone lecture
NFWI/NFU 'Caring in the Countryside' Conference
NFWI – Wales receives Good Health Wales award
WI/Bridgemere Chelsea Gold Medal for 'The Woodland
Garden'

1994 'Caring for Rural Carers' survey published
WI Markets and *Home and Country* 75th Anniversary
'Forum for the Future' conference, Denman
First WI National bowls Tournament
1995 WI member Mrs L Hacket-Pain elected World President
ACWW (Associated Country Women of the World)
'Denman Fanfare' A musical spectacular of the Denman
story

NFWI CHAIRMEN

		WIs
1917	Lady Denman DBE	
1946	Countess Albemarle DBE	6,411
1951	Lady Brunner OBE, JP	7,710
1956	Lady Dyer JP	8,296
1961	Mrs Gabrielle Pike CBE, JP	8,517
1966	The Marchioness of Anglesey DBE	8,864
1969	Miss Sylvia Gray CBE	9,051
1974	Alderman Mrs Pat Jacob JP	9,310
1977	Mrs Patricia Batty Shaw CBE, JP	9,299
1981	Mrs Anne Harris CBE	9,306
1985	Mrs Agnes Salter	9,242
1988	Mrs Jean Varnam OBE, JP	9,108
1991	Mrs Susan Stockley	8,977
1994	Mrs Elizabeth Southey	8,496

APPENDIX II

GLOSSARY OF WI TERMS

ACWW Associated Country Women of the World, to which all WIs are affiliated.

Annual Meeting Held by every WI to elect the officer and committee and to review its finance and year's work.

Annual Report of NFWI A copy is sent to every WI in March/April of each year.

'Any Other Business' Name of the guide to running a WI.

Bursary Money allocated from WI or Federation funds, or from an outside organisation, to pay for a member to attend educational courses at Denman College or elsewhere.

Certificate Organiser A member selected by her Federation to help members to attain home skills and vocational certificates.

CFWI/IFWI County Federation/Island Federation of Women's Institutes.

Constitution and Rules for Women's Institutes The legal document for WIs to be held by WIs.

Council Meeting Held by each Federation once or twice a year to review work and finance.

Dual Membership Open to a WI member wishing to participate in the activities of a second or third WI.

General Meeting A meeting of the National Federation open to all members as explained in the Memorandum and Articles of the NFWI.

Group A collection of WIs formed in an area to arrange meetings, classes and social activities; in some counties, known as Districts.

IGM Intermediate General Meeting. Any Annual General Meeting other than the Triennial General Meeting.

Mandates Resolutions passed by the members at a General Meeting giving the Executive Committee instructions on how they wish to act.

Memorandum and Articles of Association The legal constitution of the NFWI detailing its character, powers, rights and duties.

National Council Meets twice a year. Comprises the National Executive and Federation Chairmen and Treasurers.

National Executive Committee Committee members are elected triennially by Federations and WIs to manage the funds and carry out the policy of the WI.

NFWI National Federation of Women's Institutes.

NFWI News A monthly Newsletter available to all members.

Non-Party Political/Non-Sectarian The character of the organisation is non-sectarian and non-party political, but in order to achieve the objects of the WI, this shall not be so interpreted as to prevent WIs from concerning themselves with matters of political and religious significance, provided the organisation is never used for party-political or sectarian purposes.

'On With the Show' An NFWI Handbook for Exhibitors, Judges and Show Committees.

Overseas Affiliate A woman, normally resident outside England, Wales, Jersey, Guernsey and the Isle of Man who has paid a special fee, for certain benefits, to the National Federation to retain links.

Pooling of Fares A central fund to pay delegates' expenses to the General Meeting. All WIs contribute a fixed amount.

RSC Regional Sports Co-ordinator. A WI member who facilitates and promotes sporting opportunities available to WI members on a regional basis.

'Speaking Out' An NFWI Handbook containing an indexed list of every mandate passed at an NFWI general meeting.

Tellers Impartial people brought in to count votes in a secret ballot.

TGM The first Annual General Meeting of the Incorporated National Federation in 1991, and every subsequent third Annual General Meeting.

VCO/VIO Voluntary County Organiser, or Island Organiser. A trained member available to help set up new WIs, and assist WIs in all ways.

VCMO Voluntary County Market Organiser. A person trained to help with setting up and maintaining the high standard of WI Markets.

VEC Voluntary Education Co-ordinator. A trained member whose rôle is to provide an education link at Federation level.

WI Associate An Associate of NFWI and of her local County or Island Federation of WIs.